AT THE SAME TIME

I dedicate this book
to each of the seven children
I have been privileged
to bring into this world
AND
my thanks
to each person
who touched my life,
whether the lesson was
easy to swallow or hard to accept…
~

You have all been my teachers
and I thank each one of you.

Please note, even though everything in this book is true, it is written from my perspective. We each have our own viewpoints and I respect the fact that the viewpoints of others may not agree with mine.

Many of the names have been changed.

AT

THE SAME TIME

A Medicine Woman's

Journey

Daisy Lucas

Cover art by Daisy Lucas
Cover design by Quinn Lucas

Library of Congress Control Number: 2008909373
ISBN: 978-0-615-25277-3

Printed in the United States of America via Lulu Press
(www.lulu.com)
Publisher: Daisy Lucas   atthesametime@cableone.net

Author's contact information: atthesametime@cableone.net
Author's website: www.atthesametime.net

CONTENTS

PART ONE

TRANSITION

PART TWO

MOVING FORWARD

THE STORY OF ALEXANDER

PART THREE

This is not my story,

it is that of the Creator,

my Beloved Spirit,

and I dedicate it to that Presence,

whom I love more than anyone

or anything else.

Part One

"Only He can truly lead

From

Deep, deep, deep

Within your soul

Where lie the strings of character

To be played upon by Him."

Attributed to Saint Germain

INTRODUCTION

Many years ago a space was created – a room – a work of art - a masterpiece. I wanted to create a place of absolute harmony, a place where people were surrounded by Spirit, where they could elevate to a higher level. This incredible work of art would be for everyone, where the burdens of this world could be shed while their spirit was encompassed by sound and beauty; where all the senses were awakened as the atmosphere penetrated into every cell, into every particle of their being. Basically it would be a work of art for the transformation of man. But it was only an idea in my mind. How could this possibly be created? It was a passionate, heartfelt desire; but with no clue as to how to actualize it, gradually it faded into my sub-conscious to arise only vaguely from time to time. On some level, though, the seed of this incredible creation was planted.

How did this desire to create such a space come in the first place? What was it I touched in Nepal, in India, in my heart? What was it that woke up? Where did this desire to do something to change the consciousness of mankind come from? And what would it take to learn how to manifest it?

Chapter 1

AWAKENING THE REALITY

I was a strange child who loved to dance in the graveyard on the way to school. To my parent's eyes - the eyes of atheism - I seemed merely to be a happy girl who made odd choices but who knows what is in the mind of a child, full of innocent joy and connectedness? What child has not imagined they were from another place, another time? Where does magic get lost? The innate sense there exists so much more to life than the obvious?

I must have been seven years old when I read the Rupert Bear annuals. These were wonderful English comics about a bear and his friends, Bill Badger and Algy Pug who together went on many imaginative adventures full of wonder and magic, pixies and intrigue. They were beautifully illustrated, easy to read and they drew me in. The one having the most impact was a story about wishing on a blue moon, those wishes coming true - it was great food for a young child's imagination. But ..... was it merely imagination when I began to experience the sight of blue moons for myself and again when I wished not just to be pretty when I reached sixteen years old, but also for world peace? And was it merely imagination as I felt those wishes for peace turn into prayers? Was it imagination? Was it a way to bring spirituality into the mind of a child born into an atheist, intellectual family: or was it something MUCH bigger, reaching into me, telling me to *stay* awake? Don't forget who you are even in a family where no belief in God was taught, encouraged or even acknowledged beyond being a "crutch" for people who needed something to believe. It was an environment where I was taught people had faith in something only because they were not strong enough to accept the "reality". There was nothing beyond what our physical senses could perceive and science could prove.

I was given the gift of growing up in Cornwall, an exquisite area in the South West of England. There were small villages with cottages and often quaint row houses; beautifully kept gardens full of flowers, both wild and cultivated. I loved the narrow, winding lanes, especially when they were completely canopied by trees and lined by Cornish hedges (rock walls abundant with greenery, wild flowers and life). Many areas were green, lush and serene while other parts were windswept, wild and forlorn. I was never far from the ocean with its wild, enticing cliffs and the pounding drama of the Atlantic coast; and just forty miles away the often glassy smooth surface of the English Channel. The sounds I grew up with were the mews of seagulls, the wind, the gently falling rain and silence. My mother taught me how to listen to the silence. She would sometimes quietly say "can you hear it?" I would ask "What?" and she replied "The silence .... just stop and listen". And we would stand there together, listening. Then there were the scents - the salt, rich smell of the ocean filling my nose, the pungent, but somehow pleasant odor of cows; the wild flowers. In Truro, where I spent most of my childhood, I often strolled down a narrow lane, past some cows to sit by a small waterfall - out of town, far away from other people. Nature was where I found peace, where I felt connected and had a sense of belonging not present elsewhere.

It is hard to describe the pain being raised atheist; even though my mother taught me the magic of pretending seeds were fairies and shared the love of silence. Neither good nor bad, it was just a part of my journey - being spiritually sensitive in a place where spirituality was totally denied. What I KNEW inside was ridiculed and I was subtlety put down as if I were not quite as smart as others of my family. I was raised in a physically beautiful place, by parents who were wonderful people, who loved me and stayed together, but the knowledge that life was bigger than the physical was denied me. To have the very essence of who we are looked down upon, and to be thought of as stupid and weak was not just a matter of being misunderstood; it was horrendous. In fact I experienced a great deal of fear. Not only fear of the dark, but also fear of dead things. I had some truly horrific nightmares; I was always being chased in my dreams by beings trying to kill me. Finally, by learning to fly, I could escape - but fear was still a large part of my daily reality.

Even as I walked to my stream, to my thinking place by the little waterfall, I was scared of the cows and would pass them timidly hoping they wouldn't notice me. Sometimes as I crossed the fields, I would glance around, and if the cows weren't too close I would bend over to pick buttercups and clover. The buttercups I would hold under my chin and if they reflected yellow it meant that I liked butter; from the clover I picked the tiny petals to suck out the sweet nectar. In those precious moments all thoughts and fears were gone.

The little waterfall was peaceful, but I was too scared to cross it, even though there was a log going over. I am talking about a *little* waterfall, probably only 18 inches high! I felt at peace by the water but with limitations. I sat there hour after hour, for many an afternoon, fooling myself into believing that I was content, even though the woods beyond were obviously far more interesting than the rock on which I sat.

My bedroom was in the attic, way at the top of an imposing three story house; my parent's room being on the ground floor. For a while my brother's room was also in the attic and even though it stank, (if you have experienced

3

the smell of dirty socks emanating from a teenage boys room, you know what I mean!) at least someone else was close. But when he wasn't there, I experienced waves of terror as I climbed the narrow, steep staircase up to my room. The low door appeared threatening and led to a dark, creepy space packed with boxes and trunks filled with old items – furs, christening dresses, my grandmother's old clothes. As I grew a little older, I learned to overcome some of my fears to discover many unique clothes. However, I grabbed what I wanted and exited quickly.

By the time I turned thirteen I was Deborah to my family, Daisy to my friends. I knew I could not tell anyone what was going on inside of me. I was hearing voices and spirit world was obvious. It was scary. For a while I thought I was going insane and I learned to close it off. By fourteen or fifteen, I called myself all atheist and effectively denied myself just to fit in; I "fell asleep" - and there I remained until I turned seventeen.

Late one evening, a torrential rain pounded from the darkening sky. The usual rain in Cornwall was a soft, gentle mist that gently caresses you, but this was different - it was a loud, driving rain making it hard to see through the blurred windshield even though the wipers were working their hardest. I was pulling out of my friend's driveway and could just make out her face as she waved goodbye through the downpour. Putting the car in first gear I pulled forward up the steep slope towards the main road, making the decision to turn right taking the back road through Lanner. As I waited to make sure it was safe to pull out, I heard a voice in my mind.

"You had better put on your safety belt, as you are going to have an accident." There was nothing clouding my vision and I dismissed my inner guidance with the thought, "I can't hear voices." - How could I possibly hear something which I worked so hard to convince myself did not exist? By the grand age of seventeen my young ideals of open "awakeness" had already been swallowed up. Hearing voices did not fit the reality in which I lived. I didn't listen and of course, I didn't put on my seatbelt.

Driving thirty miles an hour heading home, listening to the soothing music from the radio, I ignored the voices in my head. The road was quiet and I enjoyed the intense rain, when, all of a sudden, there was a horse in front of the car! I almost swerved into the other lane, but at that exact moment a car was coming in the opposite direction. In my adrenaline-induced, slow-motion awareness, I saw children in the back seat. I made the conscious decision to keep going straight resulting in my parent's car being demolished from the inevitable impact of the horse. There was a crash, more a dull thud, with a sickening feeling of dread.

I managed to park the car and waited, desperately watching, to see if the horse would move, willing it to get up, but, no such luck. A young girl, seven or eight years old flew out of the house followed by her Dad. She was screaming in terror - her world was no longer the same, and mine was shaken to the core though the music surrealistically continued to play as if nothing had changed.

I *had* heard a voice, it had warned me about what was going to happen. It was totally a freak accident. This horse had made the supreme sacrifice so that I would learn to listen. I could have avoided a great deal of pain over the next thirty-five years had I listened to that voice, but if I had been able to listen, I wouldn't have needed the lesson would I?

Within the next few months two other paradigm shifts occurred. The first time I had taken some LSD. This was 1970, and though I only did it a few times and some of those times were not particularly pleasant, this experience

5

altered my way of thinking radically. I was with some friends and we took a walk by my favorite stream, by the little waterfall I never crossed. My friends, Sandra and Pete, crossed the river easily by means of a fallen log which formed a natural bridge. They encouraged me to join them. I *could*; it surprised me. It wasn't even difficult, there was no fear blocking my way. It was not the LSD so much as the sense of being in that moment and only that moment; experiencing, not thinking about and analyzing the experience.

It was incredibly beautiful, spring, the woods fairy-like and delicate. The green of the leaves still new and vibrant as I came across a clearing filled with bluebells and sunlight. I breathed deeply, absorbing the colors, scents and stillness. I learned barriers and limitations created in my mind do not have to stop me.

The second shift was even more profound, my mind separated from my body. I was in my bedroom, completely outside of my body, looking down at myself. At that moment, I *knew* even if my body were dead, "I" would still exist. Many people have had similar experiences – through meditation, journeying, near death or other means. But for me, having been raised to believe death was the final experience, this was mind blowing. The fabric of "reality" of my life's understanding was beginning to unravel. Not only did guiding voices exist, but my mind would exist even after my body disintegrated. Life could never be the same, unless I chose to simply deny my experiences or to frame them as "imagination". That was not a possibility.

I felt alone; my family wasn't a place I could safely share my new knowledge. I had friends but I was so shy. Having no idea how to fill myself, I spent hours by the ocean. I loved winter in Cornwall, empty of tourists, the beaches mostly to myself. I often sat on the cliffs, spray blowing through my hair, dampening my skin. The ocean washed my lonely tears, cleansing my being, enabling me to rest my spirit in her incredible power. I shared her humor when she soaked me. My mind wandering elsewhere failed to notice a larger than usual wave heading my direction. She was my friend, my mother and grandmother; comforting me, sharing her wisdom.

Chapter 1

HIDDEN BEAUTY

One white flower, tiny but radiant, grew amidst the cracks in the wall. The gray wall lined the side of a gray street. Gray, uniformly arranged trees sat against the gray sky, as if life had been drained. Did I see the beauty of the flower? No! I was so lost in my bleak, gray world I didn't notice the flower at all. It was there, radiant for all to see. Yet, all I saw were gray bricks, gray concrete; no tiny miracle of life.

I was 19 having spent 3 months in Plymouth Art College. Plymouth, in the Southwest of England, was not far from my precious Cornwall, but it felt light years away. The art school appeared dark and unfriendly. Instead of encouragement, I found rejection. One professor disliked my style of drawing so immensely he thoughtlessly blurted out "I hate the way you draw". Feelings of devastation dropped me like a stone; amazing the impact one diminishing sentence had. It was my first foray out into the world. The dogs of dread began to circle.

One bright spot lit my world - a colorful "head shop". I loved the uniqueness of the clothes and the heady smell of incense. The bright, flowing skirts and dresses from Pakistan with little mirrors sewn into them enticed me. The rich odor and the sensuous fabrics were quite unlike anything I experienced growing up in Truro. The owner of the store, Alan, saw something in me I had not been able to see myself. He understood I was learning internally and he valued it. The first time I walked through the door, his penetrating gaze fixed me, he declared to his friend Paul, "Here's one." Seeing my bewilderment he elaborated, "I can tell by your eyes." I didn't know what he meant but my conversations with him helped me acknowledge my spiritual experiences as real.

It didn't hurt that he had dark, gypsy, romantic looks. His wavy hair falling into soft curls below his shoulders. He and Paul did their best to elevate me out of my funk. Due to their encouragement I realized I could leave the art college where I was so unhappy, find an apartment and manage on my own. Alan had never been to college, lived in a caravan and owned his own business – it was a totally different way of functioning in this world.

But even though I was friends with him and Paul, I didn't fit into their social circle. This became brutally apparent as I left the house of some of their friends, only to return when I realized I left something behind. I overheard them talking about me, how I did not fit into their group and they did not want me around. Even those whom I had considered friends were not. I felt lonely, dejected and my environment became sad and gray once again. Again, I allowed the power of words to hurt me.

The profound simple beauty of a flower helped me wake up. Not just the flower but also a friend who accompanied me. Who was willing to help me find beauty inside, at least to point me in the right direction. John, whom I had just met, was not as blind as I. All *I* could see was the ugly wall, yet this person I was with didn't notice the gray at all – he saw only the perfection of one tiny bloom, nothing else. He delightedly pointed to the flower and I was struck by the fact he saw it when I did not. My inability to find the flower on my own sickened me. I desperately wanted to see its beauty, I *needed* to see it, to feel it. A precious gift I'd once had was missing and I would do anything to get it back. I asked John how he managed to see the flower when I could not. He told me of his hitchhiking trip to India a couple of years before. Not only that, but he would be willing to do it again if I wanted to go! YES! Finally, I had purpose; amazing what having a goal can do for you! I spent the next few weeks waitressing to earn the money to travel to India saving $240.00.

Late one night, I walked in the pouring rain alone; everything seemed so alive, clean, refreshed. Reflections of lights on the rain-soaked streets shone in a glorious myriad of colors. Drops of water streamed down my face, drenching my hair. I splashed in puddles and raised my arms to welcome this new dance of life. Playing with the water, I laughed aloud joyfully.

We decided to leave England in the fall. I spent my summer back in Cornwall, in a small caravan parked in a field in an isolated area near the village of Zennor, close to Lands End. There is a wild beauty in the bleakness of that area; the rocks are etched by the wind, the clouds so close that the moisture blows right out of them. The twisted roots of heather gnarled and ancient, the yellow gorse bringing a joyful, warm light to the hills. It is desolate yet alive and vibrant. Cliffs plunge dramatically to the wild ocean below, embracing hidden coves with enticing virgin sand – unreachable – except for the seagulls. I was envious of those birds whose footprints left trails in the sand. I wished that I, too, had access to private, pristine beauty and could leave my own signature there. Cornwall gave me one more gift of its beauty that summer, yet hidden in the wrapping was again an awareness of my own limitations.

Another opportunity was offered to me – a dear friend, James (who taught me to play the flute) invited me to spend the autumn in Germany – in the Black Forest. Exactly why I chose to hitchhike to India with John, someone I barely knew, instead of travelling with a close friend I am not sure. Sometimes you have to simply follow your heart, not take the logical, easy choice.

TRANSITION

EUROPE

I was twenty years old by the time we left England in October, 1973. It was odd; I didn't feel anything – just a void: no sense of loss, no fear, no expectation - nothing. At the time, there was almost a highway from Europe to India, many people were traveling in the same direction and you could meet up in certain places (especially in the cities where you would get a visa to travel to the next country). Sometimes you met someone who would feed you or offer somewhere to stay; sometimes you went hungry and slept in the cold. I travelled light. I was not particularly strong physically so I carried only what I needed. I took my flute, one book – Siddhartha by Hermann Hesse, a change of clothes, extra underwear, my passport and a sleeping bag. It all fit into one small red flowered bag (apart from the sleeping bag which I tied on the bottom).

John and I traveled through Belgium and Germany, arriving in Munich during Oktoberfest. With the assistance of a little beer and a large German man, I was literally swept off my feet dancing the waltz! I wondered if we would survive the autobahn, the main German highway. Death was here, I was certain of it. We swerved around sharp bends at incredible speeds with dramatic drop-offs to one side. I held my breath having my first experience of prayer. Surprised I lived, we travelled on to Austria and then Yugoslavia.

Yugoslavia was bitterly cold at night; the only place we could find to sleep was on the dirt floor of a run-down shed. I lay in my sleeping bag, the cheapest I had been able to find on my limited budget. The cold crept deeper and deeper through my sleeping bag and my skin until it penetrated my bones. I was most grateful for the warming sun's appearance the next morning which was graciously accompanied by numerous birds; it amazed me how many magpies there were that morning.

Across the border from Yugoslavia was Greece, and it was with Greek people that my heart started to open. While sitting under a fruit tree eating a simple lunch of bread and cheese, someone approached us; my first thought being I must be trespassing. In England if you were caught on another's property you were considered a trespasser, but in Greece, under the pure blue sky, with temperatures that surrounded us like a gentle blanket – we were welcomed.

The elderly, gentle-faced stranger greeted us and offered us fruit from his tree to enhance our meal. I could hardly believe such generosity; I never experienced it before. I thought he probably gave us the fruit so we would leave quickly, but it was not so. The lines around his eyes etched deeply into his tanned face showed how often he smiled in his life. His eyes sparkled. He couldn't speak English, but using gestures and the expressive quality of his face, he told us we were welcome to stay as long as we wished. My heart cracked open a little during the time spent in his company.

We were still with him as the sky gradually darkened, losing its azure brilliance, the color deepening into an almost inky black. Our new friend, Matthias, no longer a stranger, took us to a restaurant where he treated us to a feast of squid and ouzo. As I cut into this supposed delicacy, black ink, dark as the night sky seeped across the plate. I was grateful for the strong liquor as it enabled me to swallow the tentacles in front of me. By the last bite, the squid it was fortunately no longer recognizable.

The passion of the Greek people, along with their generosity of heart, was clear. A verbally and physically intense argument broke out in the restaurant. It amazed me how quickly the argument became volatile and also how quickly it dissipated. This certainly was not England!

I was still pretty drunk from the ouzo as John and I headed to the beach to sleep. We met a fellow traveler, a young blond man from France; he was escaping from having to serve in Vietnam and was wandering somewhat aimlessly, not able to return to his homeland. I was very drunk and stupidly had sex with him: the next morning waking up with a horrible case of cystitis. I had to find a drug store for some medication. This was a real challenge. Trying to describe what was wrong and what I needed with hand signals was in a way funny, but the damage I caused to my friendship with John because of my sexual encounter was no laughing matter.

From Greece, John and traveled on to Istanbul which is considered the Gateway to the Orient. John wanted to fulfill his goal and reach India as quickly as possible, but I had never been out of Europe and I wanted to savor each moment. We steadily liked each other less and less, but he was really very kind and stuck with me even though I had been so oblivious to his feelings. He had promised to get me to India doing his best to make that happen.

The richness of Istanbul was so filling that any awareness of the reality of our deteriorating relationship was dulled, at least in my mind. Aromas, sounds of the market, languages, Turkish writing, domed mosques – everything was so different to me, exotic and stimulating. The tastes were incredible, real Turkish delight (a soft, delicately .flavored candy) and tiny cups of thick, dark coffee. Turkey was a feast for my physical senses rather than anything spiritual.

We stayed in Istanbul a few days and then took the Orient Express (a train ride of several days crossing Turkey) to Erzurum where we got our visas for Iran. I was experiencing diverse cultures. A blast of one country was rapidly followed by another, a quick taste and then on to the next. The train ride helped me begin the process of slowing down as we travelled into Asia leaving Europe behind.

IRAN

Iran surprised me. This was 1973, a time when the Shah of Iran was still in charge of the country, before the more fundamentalist government took over. At that time you could still see the faces of Iranian women – especially in Tehran which was quite a modern city. There was a mix of people, Christian as well as Muslim; and while most women wore scarves on their heads, their faces were left uncovered.

What surprised me the most was hitchhiking. Within minutes of lifting our thumbs in Iran, someone inevitably stopped to pick us up – usually it was the first person to drive by. Not just that, but we were given somewhere to stay and provided with food. When you travel, you learn to eat when you can as you never know when the next meal will turn up. In Iran we ate plenty!

The first ride was from a young man, slightly older than we were. He insisted on buying us dinner and paid for us to stay in a cheap hotel, though it was obvious he didn't have much money. I was not sure about his motives, so I kept my door locked. Every so often I saw his head pop up in the glass at the top of the door, jumping up to have a quick glance. I didn't sleep very soundly that night, though in retrospect, if he had intended to do me any harm, he had every opportunity. I think he was just fascinated by a Western woman. Whatever his thinking, when he offered to drive us further the next day we declined.

As soon as we put our thumbs out again, we got another ride. This time, the man was a little older exuding a feeling of trust. He generously took us to his family's house where we were hosted for the next five days. The family and extended family all lived in a small, white-washed house: mother, father, uncle, aunt and lots of kids. We were welcomed completely. They went to a great deal of trouble to shift around their sleeping arrangements to accommodate us. Obviously Bahmard was not wealthy, but he would not think of doing anything less than treating us as honored guests. He even took us to the orchard of one of his relatives so he could treat us to fresh fruit.

Bahmard had opium which the men routinely smoked. The women did not join in, but since I was Western, I was offered some. This was one reason we stayed for so long, I stupidly smoked some, got sick as a dog and couldn't travel. Bahmard and his kind, loving family took care of me until I recovered, sharing their food and their space. Five days was a long time to feed two extra mouths, but they never made us feel as if we were a burden. Even when I was better, they still didn't want us to leave.

I experienced the same generosity of heart with the Iranians as I had with Greek people. The women cared for me, (though they were somewhat amused by my opium-induced vomiting) and the children were fascinated by the two of us. It was not every day they had the opportunity to host western guests doing it with great love. I appreciated the harmony this extended family managed to create.

Inevitably, the time came to move on; Bahmard gave us a ride to Mashad. Here we acquired our visas for Afghanistan. From Mashad we took a bus to the Iran/Afghanistan border.

AFGHANISTAN

The journey I took externally can no longer be taken now. The government of Iran has changed dramatically. Though I doubt the generous heart of the people has. Afghanistan has been through excruciating pain. At the time of my journey, the Soviets were building roads in Afghanistan: I had the impression the Afghanis were grateful for help, not realizing the Soviets were simply preparing to invade. After the failed Soviet invasion, Afghanistan was left in chaos, in a state of civil war. Because of the unrest, the fundamental Taliban came into power and terrorists made their base there (the vast majority of the terrorists were not Afghani; they were simply taking advantage of the situation).

The Afghanistan I knew was simple and full of faith. I later heard that even when the Soviets were bombing Afghanistan, every sunrise and sunset those wonderful, pure-hearted people put aside fighting or hiding and bowed down in their prayer ritual. In the midst of the terror of battle they never forgot their faith. But to understand the Afghanistan I experienced, we need to wipe away what we know of Afghanistan's suffering, wipe away recent news reports and return to an easier time.

As I walked across the border from Iran to Herat, Afghanistan, I felt I had stepped back five hundred years. The mud-daubed houses were the color of the surrounding land, everything simple and timeless. The Afghani people were not curious about us the way the Iranians had been; they remained aloof – I don't mean that in a negative way at all – their demeanor radiated a self-confident calm and commanded respect. They just kept their distance.

I stayed in Herat for a week allowing myself to slow to the rhythm of Afghanistan. Herat beat to a steady pulse that permeated the atmosphere..... the hammering in the distance .... the pace of people walking .... two men drawing water from a well. Everything was acted out to the same rhythm. One man would draw a little water while the other watched, then they would both work together for a short while, finally leaving the job undone, but without any obvious concern. To me, the whole scene was hilarious, but there was a harmony about it, everything moving together as if choreographed to a drum beat in the background which set the pace; the same, slow, rhythmic pace which I also gradually slowed into.

The faces of the old men in the tea rooms showed great depth of character, wisdom and pain. Their life experiences had been carved into their skin by the brutal Afghani weather. And though they remained distant they were neither cold nor unfriendly. Candy was provided with tea instead of the sugar I was used to. When I appeared confused I was shown how to suck on the candy while drinking the tea to sweeten it; but the men would quickly return to their conversation, not overly interested in me.

There were some signs that we were not actually living in the past. There were trucks, not many, brightly decorated with flowers all over. A policeman, with a mismatched uniform, directed traffic while standing on a circular platform at the center of a four-way crossing. There was virtually no traffic in Herat, but in this instant, two trucks arrived from different directions. Only in Afghanistan could there be a traffic jam with two trucks and a policeman in pink pants!

Women were covered from head to toe by black burqas, even their eyes were covered by a crisscrossed grid of cloth through which they could see out; but no-one could see in. No-one could see their beauty. Now, since Afghanistan has been in the news, we are aware this is how Afghani women dress, but in 1973 I had no idea in some cultures women were so shielded. It must have been just as strange to them to see a young woman, uncovered and traveling alone. I was not covered completely, I still wore my denim jeans but I did my best to dress modestly and was treated with respect by the Afghani men.

It was in Herat, John and I parted ways; the pain I caused him magnified and we truly could not stand being together. I was in Afghanistan, alone, and pretty much terrified, but what choice did I have? I was not close to an embassy or an easy way back to England; it was either go forward to India or at least to Kabul, which had an embassy, or head back through Iran. I decided to go forwards. There was also something about Afghanistan that fascinated me and I wanted to experience more. I am very grateful to John – he took me just far enough to where the only way to go *was* forward and though I was alone, the road to India was filled with people traveling.

Instead of taking the bus straight to Kabul along the easier southern route, I decided to travel the Northern route via Mazar-i-Sharif, where, as yet there were no roads. Few people wanted to go that way but I was fortunate and met a young German traveler, Franz, who wanted the same experience. We joined a jeep heading North out of Herat. I had purchased an old, threadbare carpet in Herat to sleep on: every Afghani owns a carpet which they carry with them when they travel serving as mattress, prayer rug and sofa all in one. Mine was worn out, but the price was right.

I am not sure how many people were crammed into the back of that old jeep. All were Afghani apart from the two of us. Many times the road (actually non-road) was so bad we had to get out and walk. Sometimes, even then, the terrain was nearly impassable! Many areas I couldn't make out any tracks, the "road" being totally indistinguishable from the surrounding land; I have no idea how the driver navigated through the rocky, barren terrain.

Our faces were soon caked in thick dirt blowing in from the open back of the jeep. I envied the Afghani men who used the ends of their turbans to protect themselves from the onslaught of dust and I appreciated their gestured advice I wrap something over my nose and mouth so I could at least breathe. A camaraderie developed between us and after about an hour it no longer mattered that we were Western and they were Afghani, we were the same in our thick coatings of dust.

We stopped at a caravanserai to sleep; I realized why Afghani people carry their own carpets. There were places to rest, all together in one large area, but there were no beds or padding provided. We simply lay down our rugs on the hard-packed earth. We were the only Western people I saw in this part of Afghanistan and I was probably the only uncovered woman for hundreds of miles, but still the Afghani people were respectful, I felt safe in their company.

My feeling of safety was probably a little naive considering there were bandits in the areas we travelled. I found out at the end of the trip the jeep that left the week before never reached its destination. It had been raided with no word of its occupants.

My journey consisted of constantly challenging both my own shyness and my fears. I was scared of just about everything – heights, slipping, spiders, other creepy creatures, the dark, dogs, being alone...... I am amazed I took this trip – but the needs of my spirit obviously outweighed any other considerations. The lesson of the little waterfall in Cornwall was always with me, and while I may have had limits and fears, they were only on one level. On another level I possessed the ability to not be ruled by them.

The jeep stopped at a village about halfway between Herat and Mazar-i-Sharif for a few of days, enabling us to rest our sore behinds. Open stalls displayed bountiful supplies of dried fruit, and even though flies were everywhere, the fruit was incredibly delicious. I thoroughly enjoyed every bite, oblivious to any sickness.

In the early evening I took a walk, alone, to the outskirts of the village, climbing a barren hill which over-looked a riverbed. There was some water, the land was parched. But I was beginning to find beauty in the very starkness of it. I observed several Afghani men approaching the river. They reverently washed their arms and then bowed in prayer. From where I was sitting, high above the village, no sound reached me, but I could *feel* the faith of these people. It was palpable. Faith expressed by a group united in prayer was not something I had previously experienced and I watched in silence and awe.

I was totally absorbed when an eagle slid through the air not a foot away from my head. I was so still that I heard it "cut" the air as it passed, remaining in awe until it was almost dark and I needed to return to the village. This incident has never left me and I carry in my heart a deep love for Afghanistan and its people. I also hold a gratitude for their faith which helped to awaken another part of me.

In more recent years, the village is most likely destroyed, many of its occupants killed, maimed or at the very least having to live with a loss of innocence. With the pain and horror war leaves behind. I would no longer be able to climb my hill for the danger of land mines. In my heart, the beauty and simplicity of that time remains intact,

I am sure the Afghani men still make their way to the river to pray. I hope they are still watched over by the eagle.

We left the village continuing north. A couple of days later we joined the paved road being built by the Soviets. We finally arrived in Balkh in Northern Afghanistan close to the Russian border. There were Russian soldiers everywhere. My main memory of Balkh is not the Soviet presence, but the bathroom floor and the tiles on the bathroom wall. I saw rather a lot of the bathroom as I was so sick with dysentery. I was immobilized and could not move as far as the bedroom to find somewhere comfortable to sleep. I seriously thought I was going to die, and part of me wished I would. I wondered if some-one this sick could recover, but eventually I was well enough to travel and we caught a bus to Kabul. I probably should have stayed in Balkh until I was a bit stronger, but my visa was only for a month and I had already been in Afghanistan for three weeks; I had to keep moving.

During the bus ride I barely made it from bathroom stop to bathroom stop, bathroom being a VERY polite way to put it. From time to time, the bus pulled up at a field where several small pits had been dug. I inelegantly squatted over my pit while the other passengers did the same, all in close proximity. The Afghani women had a distinct advantage as their clothes were wide and long enabling them to maintain some degree of modesty. I, on the other hand was not dressed so conveniently, but I was so sick I cared very little. That bus ride was pure hell. The pit stops were not very regular. In between I just had to maintain, sinking into a nauseated cold sweat, holding in toxins that desperately sought release.

At last, Kabul where I started to feel somewhat better, though still weak. Kabul was quite a modern city and it surprised me when, for the first time, I saw the face of an Afghan woman. The young people were adopting Western ways; some of them choosing to go uncovered. We met one young female medical student who invited us to her family's house for a meal. We were treated to a delicious feast of rice cooked with meat and raisins. A large plate of food was placed in the center of a low table from which we all ate with our hands. I was informed you only eat with your right hand as you use your left hand to wipe yourself after going to the bathroom. Fortunately I was taught this lesson in Afghani etiquette before I started my meal or I would have greatly offended everyone there.

Kind as people were, I decided I preferred the country to the city. I only stayed a few days but was there just long enough to experience the outdoor market where I saw exquisite, colorful dresses which were sold for the women to wear under their black burqas. It was also enough time for an elderly Afghani man to try to buy me as his third wife – definitely time to move on! I didn't believe the person with whom I was travelling, Franz, would seriously try to sell me, but just in case, I turned and quickly walked away, leaving them to their bargaining. Later Franz told me he had been offered a million afghanis (Afghan currency) for me. I felt somewhat flattered - until I found out the exchange rate, I was worth less than a hundred dollars!

From Kabul, we traveled south, the terrain changing rapidly; we dropped in altitude as the landscape transformed from arid, mountainous desolation to a fertile, lush, green valley. It was hard to believe that Jalalabad was in the same country as Herat. Perhaps it was the contrast that made it so beautiful but the green was exhilarating, refreshing and alive. The lush gentleness didn't last long, we were soon travelling through the incredible drama and precipitous cliffs of the Khyber Pass. It was easy to respect the tough, independent Afghani people who had held the British at bay during the Afghan wars maintaining a fierce pride in who they are. I felt great gratitude, love and admiration for Afghanistan.

PAKISTAN

In Peshawar, I was again alone as my companion, Franz, went his own way. I stayed at one of the many cheap "hotels" in a funky little room. It was December 1973, a time when people were hoping for Haley's comet to change reality dramatically. A buzz of excitement and expectation resonated among the people travelling. I didn't get caught up in the energy; I was trying to deal with the reality of being companionless in Pakistan.

My first rickshaw ride in Peshawar was a mixture of novelty and guilt. In Peshawar the rickshaw drivers rode bicycles that pulled a seat on wheels, which was better than India, where they ran. Most of the rickshaw drivers were unhealthy and thin and it felt wrong to be pulled along by someone who was suffering and less healthy than I. Had I not taken a rickshaw ride obviously they would not have been paid, but I was still conflicted. I found the whole reality of beggars extremely difficult to deal with, I encountered my first in Afghanistan but there were far more in Pakistan. I confronted my own discomfort and guilt.

I disliked Pakistan, I never felt safe. It was the first time I had no-one to travel with, which greatly exaggerated my discomfort. Because I was Western, the Pakistani men thought I was a prostitute. This impression Pakistani men had of women was hard to break. My jeans had worn out and been replaced by the same baggy Pakistani pants local women wore. I was careful to cover my head with a shawl but even so, stray hands would sometimes creep my way. After a couple of bad experiences where men grabbed me, I went to the embassy for advice. It was not different attire that was recommended -- it was to carry a pin. Oh! What a pleasure the first time someone thought my breasts looked inviting!

The opportunity to try my new defense mechanism came soon. I was on a bus, next to an American, when a hand came creeping around my neighbor's back towards my breast. I never saw the face of the man, but it was great fun to see the hand recoil as I stabbed it firmly and surely.

It was interesting; in Afghanistan you never saw a woman's face or body. But I felt safe and respected as a woman; I never felt threatened. Yet in Pakistan, where I was dressed much more conservatively and where women's faces were seen though their heads were covered, I was treated inappropriately.

I arrived in Pakistan on December 12th 1973 and I was relieved when I met an American couple who befriended me. The wife, Konani, was beautiful, a Hawaiian woman with long black hair coupled with deep, expressive eyes. Her husband, Ray, was a California blond whose blue eyes sparkled with a joyful passion for life. They invited me to join their journey to the foothills of the Himalayas in Pakistan for Christmas. I was extremely grateful. I knew I was heading towards India, but I felt unsafe and worried about crossing Pakistan by myself. My fear paralyzed me; I simply didn't know how to move forwards. At least the "hotel" was safe, but I needed a kick in the butt and this side trip to the mountains got me moving.

Mountain people of Pakistan were definitely mellower than people in the city, but I still felt an undercurrent of cruelty as I observed one man kicking his dog for no apparent reason. I did not feel at peace here, questioning whether I was supposed to stay.

Christmas Day, 1973, I climbed a mountain with Konani and Ray. I had a very hard time with heights, the possibility of slipping (one of the many fears I was learning to challenge). My friends climbed easily – it was actually more of a steep mountain trail than a climb – but I was terrified at every step.   With their encouragement, both verbal and physical, I made it to a high plateau – it was glorious, stunning. It was my first vision of the Himalayas.

I allowed my pounding heart to slow its frenetic pace, the unsteady feeling in my legs gradually abated. I was able to expand my view; the less fear I held onto, the more spectacular the view became. As the sun lowered towards the horizon my fears grounded, no longer affecting me. It was magical; I was awestruck as the sun reflected on the mountain deepening and intensifying in color, glowing with an inner fire.   A majestic Christmas present for a rather small and lonely girl.

Chapter 6

INDIA

After leaving the mountains, Konani, Ray and I journeyed to Rawalpindi together. Then I continued on to Lahore basically alone. For the first time I wished to move faster than my companions and on December 31st 1973, I crossed the border from Pakistan into India. On the Pakistan side, right before I crossed, a huge vulture loomed over me from a branch above my head. As I crossed into India, the energy changed. Everything lightened considerably. In my mind I felt as if I walked from hell into heaven. I stepped forwards and the old could no longer touch me. *I crossed the border, the vulture did not.*

During my trip I smoked some marijuana (both in Afghanistan and in Pakistan), but as I crossed that border into India, I knew I would not smoke any more. It was clear to me I needed to stop; drugs were no longer needed and would not be part of my life. The pollen I smoked in Afghanistan scared me as it was so strong and seemed to magnify the paranoia I felt from being on my own. It took me a really long time to "come down".

It was time for a new phase in my life and I began the new year in a new country with a new and clearer direction.

Traveling a short way into India, I arrived in Amritsar, where I stayed for three days. On the day of my arrival was a huge festival; it was a holy day, the birthday of Guru Gobind Singh. The place packed with people. Everyone in a joyful mood, full of celebration. The Sikhs offered free food to all, reason enough for many people to be happy. Dahl (a lentil dish) was served in huge leaves to many grateful, hungry mouths. Having become so sick in Afghanistan, I was wary of strangely served food, but my money was getting really low and I ate gratefully. Humbled, I sat alone in the crowd on the magnificently tiled ground, my leaf in hand.

The Sikhs were visiting the Golden Temple to pray. I was surprised and a little intimidated when I was invited to join a small group. The temple, set in the center of a spring-fed lake with a walkway leading to it was awe inspiring. The golden structure glowed in the sun, reflecting its glory into the sacred water surrounding it. Hymns were chanted to the accompaniment of flutes, drums and stringed instruments.

It was remarkable to walk down that path on my first day in India; the first day of a new year, the first day of a new direction. I walked with new purpose and greater clarity that I felt arise in me. I had watched the Afghani people from afar, but in Amritsar I was invited into the heart of the Sikh religion. I was privileged to be in the place all Sikhs want to visit in their lifetimes. No wonder I was in awe as I approached the truly magnificent Golden Temple.

The young Sikh escorting me was proud to show me this holy site, amazed I was here. Here in India! In this sacred place! But stunning as it was, it was not the external beauty that moved me, it was more the holiness and reverence. As I entered the temple, I felt the same depth of quiet energy I experienced while watching the Afghanis at prayer, palpable yet not visible. It was something these people knew and experienced on a daily basis, yet was missing in my own life. I expected the room inside the temple to seem empty and yet it didn't, there was a definite atmosphere, a serene, sublime peace. Even with the noise of celebration going on, time stopped inside the temple - just for a moment, one infinite moment.

In Amritsar I met a young Canadian man of Indian descent, Dinesh. I traveled with him to Delhi. He warned me about how people would stare openly at me, but it was still disconcerting. We ate at a very good restaurant in New Delhi (an advantage of being with Dinesh was that he knew where to find a good meal for very little money). Unlike most countries, they did not look away as I looked back at them, they just kept watching me, unabashedly, making me feel extremely uncomfortable.

Dinesh was sweet and kind, as well as being rather good looking and I attached myself to him a little too much. I was still very lost and he knew where and who he was. He held an air of absolute confidence. He was tolerant of my neediness for long enough to get me close to Nepal, his self-assuredness strengthening me. He understood the Indian people and he understood the system, helping me navigate my way through the vast numbers of people traveling on the buses and trains.

On the bus to Delhi from Amritsar people had been hanging on the sides and on the roof rack, every available hand-hold had someone hanging on to it. The train from Delhi to Lucknow (close to the Nepalese border) was similar but due to Dinesh's extensive travel experience he knew to procure a luggage rack for us – not for our luggage but for us! It was a long trip and we could sleep horizontally whereas others had to sleep sitting up. Every available spot was taken: every seat, every rack and every part of the floor.

He also taught me to put my money and passport under my head as I slept ensuring they would still be there when I woke up. Dinesh got me safely to Lucknow from where I could make my way alone into Nepal.

Chapter 7

EXTREMES

NEPAL

Nepal drew me far more strongly than India. I had managed to find one traveling companion after another, but Nepal became my own intensely spiritual and profoundly personal journey. I was on my own completely from Lucknow, but this was necessary in order to have the experiences I needed to wake up. It was also necessary for me to learn I could indeed do this by myself.

My journey into Nepal began with the wonderful Tibetan people whom I came to love deeply. I managed to secure a ride on an ancient truck – there were no other Western people, just me with about forty Tibetans, returning from a pilgrimage to see the Dalai Lama in Dharamsala. They were incredibly kind; they knew my western legs could not remain compressed as long as theirs and they were very patient each time I had to move and stretch a little. We were so squashed together, there was really no room to do anything except sit still with your legs folded under you.

I was terrified at the prospect of continuing on by myself, but these gentle Tibetan people took care of me. They spoke no English, and I spoke no Tibetan, but silently one elderly man broke off a piece of his food and handed it to me. The twinkle in his eye expressed a level of love I had not previously encountered. I believe it is true that Tibetan people only bathe once a year and I think this group must have been about due for a bath, fleas hopped visibly from one person to the next. Their hands were black, but because this ball of food (I have no idea what it was) was offered with such love, I could no more refuse to take it than I could deny how special these people were. The trip was long, several hours, uncomfortable as I was, I wished it would never end.

The fear of being alone intensified, but even though it was dusk by the time we reached Katmandu, finding somewhere to stay was easier than I thought. There were many lodges set up for tourists. Some even advertising showers. By this time I was not surprised to find the shower was a bucket filled with water, hoisted up above my head, from which I had to pull a plug to release a cold flood. I learned to wash very quickly! I also had to overcome more fears. While sleeping in a room with lizards crawling on the walls, I had to quit worrying about creepy crawlies or I would never have slept at all.

Katmandu was fascinating with its temples, carvings and noise. Everything in constant motion. As I preferred something quieter, I would often take walks into the back streets. Curious heads would turn my direction then go back to their work; children played barefoot in the streets, oblivious to the dirt, a dead goat's head sitting by the door. The rest of the goat was probably being cooked and the skin used for some container or clothing, but the head sat, useless, discarded.

One night I decided to go out late, long after the hubbub slowed. Silence descended leaving a welcomed peace. I met three beggar children; I am not sure how old they were - probably between 5 and 10 years old. I still had not found a way to resolve the emotions I felt when faced with the reality of beggars.

This time was different; the children were just happy to see me. I bought them some yogurt (delicious stuff made from water buffalo milk, which is sweeter than cow's milk) and then we walked together through the nearly silent streets. They were happy children even though their lives were hard and they seemed carefree as we danced and skipped together over the steps of the temples.

I was twenty years old and English – what a privileged life I led in comparison to these children and yet here we were hand in hand laughing and dancing. It was a moment in time when two totally different worlds touch and experience simple joy. It had been a long time since I felt like a child and it was incredible to experience lightness in my heart. I was amazed I did not feel afraid. The fear had dissipated. The moon seemed brighter and the temples walls were filled with detailed carvings I failed to notice until now. For the first time, I was simply in Katmandu, on a magical night.

Chapter 8

HIMALAYAS

I spent only a few days in Katmandu before heading into the Himalayan Mountains. There were several trails to choose from and I decided to take the trail to Jomsom taking me closest to the Tibetan border, where in my heart I wanted to go. A bus took me to Pokhara, from there, I walked. I still picture the dirt and stones as I took those first steps. I can still see the small stream I needed to ford. Almost every step challenged me to overcome barriers trying to hold me back. The night I had danced with the beggar children, when fear had not been present at all, taught me it did not have to be a constant part of me. It lessened, and was bearable.

I walked all day stopping in a simple village for the night. The villagers along the trail were used to foreigners and were happy to earn some money by feeding and housing them. I had spent my first day on my own finding I was actually enjoying it! As I woke up in the morning, the old fears tried to seep back into my consciousness. I sat by a stream running through the village, playing my flute quietly to the placid water, feeling a reflection of the water in my music. The birds joined my song lifting my spirits with their wings as they flew. Nature calmed my lonely heart, the gentle stream carried my fear away.

Though I never learned to play my flute in a traditional sense, it became an extension of me, enabling me to release my feelings and emotions. A couple of Japanese tourists passed me as I sat, two young men. I stopped playing the flute and shyly acknowledged them as they waved in recognition. For the first time I was happy I didn't have company, I felt no compulsion to run after them to see if I could join them; I was content by myself, with myself.

I began following a trail which led across a narrow bridge hundreds of feet above a raging river. I walked down, down, down, the trail descending rapidly towards the bridge leading from the village of Birethani. Though I tried to control my emotions, they raged as rapidly as the river below as I took my first nervous step onto the bridge. If I were to turn back at this point, I would never get deeper into the Himalayas, ever.

I remembered the stream I sat beside as a child, not being able to cross. But I also remembered when my perspectives changed, I could. I recalled the beauty denied me due to my reluctance to challenge my limits. I was determined not to allow that to happen again. I refused to deny myself the mysteries of the Himalayas. I focused on the other side of the bridge and step by step steadily walked towards my goal, not looking down. The bridge swung with every footfall, making me disoriented. I made it across, a little shaken, definitely in need of some deep breaths but filled with greater self-confidence.

The climb down had been steep, but it was nothing to the climb back up the other side. There were hundreds of steps carved into the rock. I trudged slowly upwards. I was so tired I took a drink from a small stream that trickled beside the path, my memories of dysentery fading as I became more and more exhausted.

Gratefully I came to a tiny village, Ulleri, and stayed at the first house I came to with a Tibetan family. The Tibetans were surprised at my request for hospitality as most people kept walking to the lodge at the top of the ridge, but I could not take one more step. Though unusual, they welcomed me. This was my first night devoid of Western people.

Late the next day, I finally arrived at the top of the ridge. It was dusk, the daylight slowly dimming, the air crisp and clear. My exhausted legs ached while I filled with exhilaration. I watched as the stars appeared; first one, then five, they kept multiplying until there were more stars than I ever knew existed. It was quiet and incredibly still. There was an inn on the ridge where I gratefully rested.

The next day I walked more slowly than any-one else and was soon passed by them all, once again by myself; but no longer feeling alone. I walked very slowly the whole trek, I appreciated every twist and turn in the trail, every flower, every blade of grass, every new smell and sight. I did not want to miss anything. When someone passed me, walking speedily, I could not help thinking they were missing something I was able to experience. I began to appreciate my solitude. In the mountains I felt safe again. All of my senses came to life. Each night the air was clearer than the night before, the stars more numerous and the silence more absolute.

I stayed at whatever village I came to at the end of the day; there was always someone ready to take in a guest to sleep on the floor around the fire with them for a small fee. Whether I was staying or just walking through, I would be offered some tea at each village. There was inevitably a tea room, however small the village, even if there were just a few simple grass-roofed houses.

Everywhere I stayed, over my two months in the mountains, the same food was served – rice, dhal and often a type of root somewhat like a potato. For two months I ate the same food every day for both daily meals, yet somehow I never got bored. The subtle differences in flavor from village to village were wonderful and I appreciated each bite. My heightened senses appreciated this simple fare more than food served in any fine restaurant.

I walked away from civilization into a simpler life and began to wake up. The further from lights, cars, soft beds, music and a variety of foods I walked, the more I found an understanding of what was truly important. My mind cleared as I walked in harmony with my surroundings. Flowers were incredibly beautiful, the scent sometimes hitting me before I knew where it was coming from; a snow eagle soared above my head calling to me. I listened to the gently flowing passage of a stream and could hear every sound. I focused and separated the watery music coming from the stream as it gently rippled over two rocks here, tumbled over seven rocks there; deeper still I heard the music of the whole.

I continued slowly along the trail to Gorepani, which at 10,000 feet is the highest pass enabling views of both Annapurna and Daulagiri. I had heard the sunrises were spectacular; purposely waking early I climbed another two thousand feet to Poon Hill to absorb the dawn. Clouds blocked the beauty others experienced but I stayed, enjoying the silence, watching the village slowly wake up. I heard the roosters, then the dogs, and gradually the people emerging from their houses; a new day had begun.

I stayed a second night in the hope of catching a more glorious sunrise, but instead was greeted by at least a foot of deep, luxurious snow. I had never experienced more than an inch before and it was magical. After the sun had risen fully, I hiked out of the village into the rhododendron forest. I walked enshrouded in a deep mist.
I stopped moving, squatting in the snow with my flute. As the crunching of my footsteps stopped, all sound ceased. The rhododendron surrounding me appeared as hands, pointing towards the ground, weighted down with their heavy burden. The silence was absolute and utterly peaceful. All color gone – only the white of the snow and the thick mist all around. Into this silence I began to play my flute, gently and softly, first the notes merely

expressing my faintest breath then becoming stronger. I did not feel I disturbed the silence, but rather my playing became part of it. Until the quiet no longer wanted the accompaniment of music, I stopped playing, the final notes absorbed by the snow.

Gradually the mist began to clear ....then out of the silence I heard bells. I thought it was my imagination, but the tinkling grew louder, soon with laughter mingled in. I sat, un-noticed, as the sound became clearer, then along the path came a Tibetan mule train. I witnessed several generations, young to very old carrying their heavy loads. The women laden with huge bundles of sticks, trudging through the deep snow. It was a hard life and yet they were happy. They crossed a narrow swinging bridge a little ahead on the trail and some of the young Tibetan men began to jump making the bridge bounce. They laughed uproariously with such absolute delight at this game the whole family joined in, young and old alike. I sat quietly until they were out of sight and I listened until the final tinkling of the bells faded, merging with the silence once more.

Winter thawed into spring as I headed down the other side of the pass, the snow gradually thinning until it was all gone. Each drop in altitude brought new delights, different flowers, butterflies, bugs and birds. I stopped half way down the trail at a village which most trekkers passed on through and stayed the night with a young Nepalese woman. I bought the shirt she had been wearing from her; it had an elegant cross-over style. It cost me very little, but to her it seemed like a lot of money, and we were both happy with the deal.

After the usual meal of rice, dhal and tea, I continued down the trail to the valley, where oranges were growing on the trees. In two days I walked from deep snow to orange and lemon groves. This was Tatopani, and

I was not the only one to appreciate the exceptional beauty of the valley which surrounded the river. Tatopani was warm and yet surrounded by enormous snow-capped peaks. It was spectacular.

There were several lodges designed for tourists – the most popular of which was owned by a Japanese man and his Nepalese wife; this was where I decided to stay.

I was now by the river's side, not high above it in the mountains. On the bank were natural hot springs; two pools, one situated above the other. I immersed myself gratefully in the hot water taking a long awaited, luxurious bath. I would have stayed for hours allowing the effects of my journey to relax out of my tired muscles, but two men were heading in my direction. Dressing quickly, I returned to the village.

The trail behind me, through the mountains, had disappeared. The spirit changed, something shifted and I harmonized with the breathtaking beauty of the Himalayas.

Late one night, I went outside, leaning against the wall above the river just breathing in the peace. Looking up at the overwhelming multitude of stars, there was more light in the sky than dark; I *knew* the certainty of God's existence. Everything was so clear. I could no longer deny the reality of God. It wasn't a question, it wasn't even faith, it was beyond that – I knew, I absolutely knew; I felt it in every part of me. There was something so huge I was part of, a Presence, far more palpable than in the Golden temple, far more profound. I was held in the myriad of stars, in absolute stillness. I knew in that timelessness it was possible to reach perfection; to be in absolute peace and harmony.

It was joyful yet also serious. I found it was harder to know the reality of God than to deny it. I realized all of my "private" thoughts weren't private. I knew Spirit understood me intimately knowing I needed to change. I saw parts of myself that were hidden not only from others, but also from myself; parts that were not pleasant, that I did not want to acknowledge. Yet all of this was known; I could no longer hide. I felt God ask if I really wanted this course – I was told it was much harder, but I answered "Yes, it has to be easier than being in ignorance." I was given the choice of where I wanted my life to go. I learned that we are *always* given a choice. Even something as fundamental as knowing Creator/Spirit/God will not be forced on us; we have to want it. I found I desperately wanted it.

I rested in Tatopani for a week, taking a couple of hikes down different paths out of the village. On one of these side trips I wandered off the used trail. There were prayer flags but no sign of people. In this isolated place, I met a Sadhu (a wandering Indian Holy man). He was fairly young with long unkempt hair and simple clothing, covered in ashes as is their tradition. We had a conversation in which he asked if I would give him my flute, not my silver one, but a wooden one which I had bought in Katmandu. He pointed out I didn't need two flutes; I agreed and happily gave it to him. My generosity surprised me as I often had a hard time parting with possessions. He smiled as he left.

Only then did I fully realize he had been speaking in Hindi (or Nepalese) and I had been speaking in English. Yet we had understood each other, not by universal gestures but we understood the words we had each spoken; we had just had a conversation! I was shown there is no language; there is a realm where language does not exist. In this new-found Presence I was starting to bring into my life, there is no separation.

At the lodge where I stayed, I met three Japanese guys (two were the young men who passed me on the trail.) and two American girls. It was good to be in the company of people who spoke English. One of the Japanese guys was heading back to Katmandu and I asked if he would take a pair of Tibetan boots (which I had bought from an elderly Tibetan) to mail to England. I didn't want to keep carrying them, I knew I would be in the mountains for a while longer.

Later, I found out, when they arrived in England with no message, just the boots, my mother thought it was the end of her youngest daughter! It was the only time my mother cried since the beginning of World War II when my Dad left for war. I did not leave the Himalayan Mountains for another six weeks; there was no mail or any other way to communicate, so all my parents knew was silence, an old pair of boots and then more silence. For me life was changing quickly, perhaps in a way it was symbolic of the death of my old life.

Mitzu and Shuto arrived in Tatopani a week ahead of me. There was something about Mitzu everyone around him loved. He had an aura of peace, his presence calm, yet charismatic; people gravitated towards him. I saw in him an ideal, he seemed to be a pool of wisdom – the kind of person I wanted to be. I needed to be around him – yet I felt unworthy. My heart ached to be with him, and even though our physical encounter was short, the impact of meeting him stayed with me for years. He was my motivation to grow, my inspiration to strive in a way I never had before. Instead of something abstract, which was a new concept for me, Spirit gave me a person who personified an ideal for me to grow towards. It helped me see what I wanted to change more clearly, in terms I could relate to.

After several days in Tatopani we, (Mitzu, Shuto [his friend] and I) traveled on towards Jomsom. At one point, rocks pounded down around us, almost hitting us as we walked the trail. I couldn't figure out what was happening. The rocks were coming from high up the cliff and on the other side was a steep drop, so they were hard to avoid. I thought I caught a glimpse of something on the side of the mountain, but it was difficult to make out among the shadows of the trees. Finally, one appeared clearly - a snow monkey making it clear he didn't like intruders in their silent land.

We continued on – mostly in silence – until we came to a place where the mountains were so exquisitely beautiful. The scent from small blue flowers saturated the air with their perfume; the bird song was pure and clear. As I walked through the blossoming rhododendron forests, I remember thinking, "This is enough, I feel 'high' enough." I believed I could not be any happier or more at peace than I felt at that moment.

We stopped in Marpha, a lovely town of white-washed houses at a little tea house. The people were wonderful, warm, welcoming, full of heart. They were not Tibetan, but a different tribe of Nepalese who were Buddhist, their physical appearance being somewhere between the Nepalese and Tibetans. At the villages back along the trail the Tibetan refugees were delegated to jobs no-one else wanted (dealing with the dead for example) and they could only live on the outskirts: not so in Marpha. There was more harmony between the Nepalese and Tibetan residents.

Mitzu decided to stay in Marpha, but I felt pulled towards Tibet. I wanted to get as close to the Tibetan border as possible, so Shuto and I walked on. The trail became ever more desolate and rugged; I never knew the wind could be so brutal. The harsh, dry grittiness blew relentlessly; sometimes so strongly I felt I would be blown down the mountainside. I peered through slitted eyes at the sandy, dusty landscape; it was virtually deserted, but I could just make out a man with a yak across the plain battling the wind in an effort to keep moving forwards. My inner thighs were chapped from the constant abrasion of dust and biting cold; but it was still exciting to see the yak, ensuring I was closer to Tibet.

Just the day before, I had washed my hair in a stream outside Marpha. It was March, the stream had been snow melt, the icy shards of water piercing my skull; luxurious compared to this. Now, my newly washed hair was full of grit, matted and blown. It slashed my face scratching my eyes as I squinted to make sure I was still on the trail. It was not far from Marpha to Jomsom but the contrast from the friendly rhododendron forest to these stark surroundings made it seem worlds apart.

Jomsom itself was somewhat forbidding. The trail continued on towards Mustang and into Tibet, but Western people were not allowed to go further than Jomsom. There were soldiers to make sure we didn't pass. The soldiers seemed a little suspicious of me.

The final point of the trail was reached; it had taken me six weeks. On the return journey from Jomsom, I realized it had been a mistake to think I was "high enough" further back on the trail. It seemed clear to me I had limited my growth somehow by my thinking. The wind seemed to have steadily eroded the "high" and now I felt distinctly lacking against the brutal starkness of my surroundings. That lesson stayed with me; it is dangerous to think you are grown enough. Our path is an eternal one always growing, learning and changing. To stagnate and think we know everything we need to is a big mistake. I learned from this to never give up until something is completed. I was conscious never to say again "That is enough" until I had done everything I could.

In retrospect I know I did not value myself, thinking someone else must deserve to feel this happy more than me. It has taken me another thirty years to learn that one! We are so very precious, each one of us and each one of us deserves to have complete happiness, and then some!

Chapter 10

RETURN

Returning to Marpha we rejoined Mitzu, definitely more bedraggled than when we left. The three of us slowly made the exquisite trek back to Tatopani. Mitzu deciding he would remain there by the hot springs. I knew I must return to Katmandu, though reluctantly; my visa had only been valid for a month and I had already been in the mountains for almost seven weeks. I didn't want to get kicked out of Nepal. Shuto accompanied me back to Katmandu. Instead of hiking through the high pass of Ghorepani, we went the gentler route following the river down the valley to Beni. It was less dramatic, but still incredibly beautiful. The landscape more serene; tiny villages dotted the green, terraced fields.

A Tibetan family, a couple with two children, who dwelt in a simple white-washed building, welcomed us. I was invited by the Tibetan man to join him on the flat roof of the house. I sat on one side while he sat a short distance away obviously praying while I read the copy of 'The Tibetan Book of the Dead' which I brought into the Himalayas with me.

I understood the book clearly - I saw how it was many different paths into the spirit world and I realized if I wanted to, I could focus on any one of the "guides" and go to that level, even the highest levels. I was shown all the paths clearly and I knew there was something else I was looking for. Sadly, I knew the Tibetan teachings were not put in my path; a great love for Tibetan people definitely, but not the teachings. I was grateful to the Tibetan man; I knew my understanding came because of his prayer for me.

We descended from the roof and were treated to Tibetan butter tea, quite different from the Nepalese tea that greeted us at each previous village. It was offered with such heart and delight by the Tibetan family; it was impossible not to enjoy it. They thoroughly enjoyed watching me trying to figure out if I liked this strange, somewhat salty taste or not, and when they added tsampa (a meal which thickened it) the taste and texture were *both* strange, though not unpleasant.

The trip out of the Himalayas was far faster than my trip in, a little too fast, and Kathmandu was a shock to my newly opened senses, both physical and spiritual. The noise and activity were overwhelming. After two months in the profound silence of the mountains, the yelling, bicycle bells and masses of people were all too intense and I overloaded.

My visa was easy to renew. I had overstayed by a month but I simply told the officials the mountains were just too beautiful to leave. I had become spiritually open and now it seemed every spirit was trying to jump into me. I lost my sense of reality. I saw a monkey at Swayambunath Temple which was obviously possessed by a spirit that was not just monkey, but more human. I felt the same was happening to me.

Kathmandu is where I met Diana again, one of the American girls I befriended in Tatopani. She helped me gain some sense of normalcy. I visited Bodnath Temple with her and holding a conversation helped me get out of the chaos in my head. Diana, Shuto, Mitzu (when he returned from the mountains) and I occasionally met in one of the tea houses designed for travelers. I avoided these before going to the mountains. It felt "wrong" to be eating french toast in Nepal, but after two months of the same food day after day it was interesting to try Nepalese versions of western food. After a while, my friends moved on and I was once again alone.

I was not yet ready to leave Nepal but I needed somewhere quieter and calmer. I decided to move slightly outside of Katmandu, close to Swayambunath Temple. That area of Katmandu Valley was across the river which stank, a mixture of rot and urine. The day I moved, at the base of the steps, on the river bank, a body was being cremated on a funeral pyre. Women were wailing as the remains were consumed in the fire. The ashes to be returned to the earth and the spirit - to find another.

All my belongings were on my back, either in my bag or tied to it - my Afghan rug, my flute, sleeping bag and my copy of 'The Tibetan Book of the Dead'. I wore my maroon, flowered Pakistani pants, but they were wearing out and I started wearing a plain orange sari I bought in Katmandu. I was uncomfortable walking past the little but intimidating Tibetan dogs. I was a stranger, preferring to be anonymous but instead was loudly announced by their yipping and barking.

It was not difficult to find a simple room to rent - a small, square room with white-washed walls. I used my Afghani rug both to sleep on and as a prayer rug and on the walls I put my newly acquired pictures - a beautiful painting of a female deity, a poster of Shiva and a poster of Ganesh. These pictures brought me much needed guidance, especially the peaceful, female deity - I didn't know who she was but she helped bring me peace. She was painted onto a piece of cloth, a white figure sitting on a lotus flower with mountains on either side, surrounded by flowers; she had eyes on her forehead, hands and feet. I was protected and calmed by her presence and the little room became a haven for me, a sanctuary. It was many, many years later I realized it was Tara; Tara who had been with me far more recently in other times of crisis. Tara, had always been there for me. She is the Tibetan deity who promises to be there for all mankind until we are released from ignorance.

There was a Tibetan tea shop in the area which I frequented. I could feel the owner's concern for me, he could easily tell I was confused, and one time when I was sitting drinking tea I could sense he was going to find me help, the type of help I didn't want. Many western travelers had ended up in a mental hospital in Katmandu and I was determined not to join them. I intuitively knew who he was going to call, and I exited the tea house rather rapidly, shaken but determined to take charge of my life.

Returning to my room, I passed an elderly Tibetan man in prayer. He spun his prayer wheel chanting all day as he walked, "Om Mani Padme Hum, Om Mani Padme Hum," the mantra of the Buddha of compassion. I tried chanting myself and it helped calm me as it gave me something to focus on. Once again, someone else's faith strengthened me.

I am not sure how long I remained in my room, chanting, communing with the pictures, simply being quiet and trying to get clear - possibly one day, possibly three or four, maybe longer, but eventually I was able to venture out. I became aware of the gift my mother had given me; I had been wanted as a child from before I was conceived; I was born at home and was breast fed. Even in the chaos I was experiencing, there was a deep, deep place of stability inside. There was a solid core inside the tempest and those contemplative days inside my room, in solitude, enabled me to commune with it.

I decided to climb to Swayambu Temple. The steps stretched up the hill above me, seemingly endless. There were monkeys everywhere, in the trees, on the path, in front of me, behind me and above me. As I ascended, I felt clearer; the steps became progressively steeper the closer I got to the top, but the harder the climb the more determined I became. Day after day I made this journey to the temple. My appreciation of those steps grew; I knew the path was hard, because at the top was a blessing. It taught me to keep going through many aspects of my life – just keep going, it *will* get better. Just as the steps got steeper sometimes things look harder, sometimes they seem near impossible, right before break through.

I accepted the support of the monks as I made a circular route around the temple; I could *feel* their prayers for me as I passed by the enormous prayer wheels. My mind in confusion and my heart yearning desperately for the peace I had known deep in the Himalayas. I listened to the rhythm of the drums and horn, cymbals and chanting, the sounds pulsed inside my very being. Resonating at the core I had touched, strengthening it. As I became stronger internally I tried to discern the meaning of the symbols around me. The monks never spoke to me, but I was immensely grateful for their prayers.

During my last sacred visit to the temple, I finally understood the meaning of a series of doorways (or gates) that were in a row in order of diminishing size, each one smaller than the one before. You had to pass spiritually through each gate. I learned that my spirit needed to be completely centered, my ego gone. At first my spirit was scattered, I could not pass through; but eventually by practicing this exercise, I was able to advance through the gates until finally I could "pass through" the smallest one.

I also used the rest room at the temple. As I eliminated, I felt all of the garbage I was carrying was washed away. You can pray anywhere, break through anywhere, even in a bathroom (in this case especially in a bathroom). It was directly symbolic of getting rid of waste I didn't need.

I walked slowly and meditatively back to my room, knowing it was finally time to leave Nepal.

EASTERN NEPAL

In order to leave Nepal, I boarded a bus heading through Eastern Nepal towards Darjeeling. I was still somewhat confused and didn't realize as a westerner I was not permitted to enter Eastern Nepal; it was a protected area and foreigners were not allowed. My clothing enabled me to pass for a rather pale Nepali, and my inner conflicts stopped me from conversing with anyone. I just paid my money and boarded the bus, totally unaware I should not be doing so. I was no longer afraid of travelling alone, which was a good thing as not only was I by myself, there were obviously no other western travelers headed that direction.

The bus stopped at a small village; I must have looked totally out of place as we all disembarked for a while, but as fate would have it, I was in exactly the right place at the right time, laws having nothing to do with it. At the bus stop was a Nepalese man, Barati, who spoke excellent English. It turned out he lived in England and was visiting his family for a short while. He obviously wondered why I was there and enlightened me to the fact I was in a restricted area.

He kindly invited me to stay with him and his family for a few days; I was relieved and grateful. My journey had taken a toll both physically and emotionally; my stomach was swollen, I had constant gut pains and was totally worn out. Barati was thoughtful and generous, I was fed well and rested comfortably. He was concerned about me, he had children in England and I think he treated me as one of his own daughters. He advised me to go straight back to England as soon as possible.

An elderly Sadhu, wearing nothing but a loin cloth and coated with ashes, visited Barati while I was there. He was considerably older than the young Sadhu I met on the trail by Tatopani. He possessed an aura of wisdom and serenity. There was obviously a great deal of respect between the two men. Barati's concern for me was shared with the Sadhu. The holy man asked to see my palm and Barati translated his message to me. "How old is your father?" he asked. I replied, "sixty years old." "This is why you are having all these difficulties" was his comment. There was something in the bearing of the Sadhu that left no room for doubt. I was left to reflect on what this could possibly mean as the two men returned to their conversation in Nepalese.

After a week of nurturing, I was stronger and it was time to move on. Before I left, Barati said to me "The Messiah will come; he will be the one to unveil the parables of the Bible". This conversation in the middle of East Nepal had very little meaning to me at the time. I had no idea what the concept of messiah meant. Christian terminology had virtually nothing to do with either my upbringing or my spiritual journey to this point, but it was a conversation I noted. He also asked me if I was serious in my quest to find truth, and reiterated what I had been told in Tatopani, that it was a much harder course than not knowing. I unequivocally replied "Yes, I was very serious." My determination to continue forward had not been abated either by my confusion or by being given a safe, comfortable rest.

He firmly repeated his opinion that I return to England, and also advised I should go to America at some point in the future. I felt no attraction to America; I loved the third world countries and dismissed the possibility from my mind quickly. He kindly escorted me to the border of Nepal towards Darjeeling and persuaded the border guards to let me through. The word 'rebel' was written on my passport, I was questioned and my pictures were examined, but after some time I was allowed to leave.

I boarded a bus from the border to Darjeeling, being treated to a glorious view of Mount Everest. So huge, the top continually wreathed in clouds. It was a magnificent goodbye gift with its grandeur, strength and absolute presence. I was struck once again by how unbelievably beautiful the Himalayas are. But though awed by Mount Everest, I knew my time in Nepal was finally over. In the four months I spent there, I found the reality of God but I also became so open that I was extremely vulnerable to spiritual confusion. Yet I knew I was undeniably protected and guided.

Perhaps I should have followed Barati's advice and returned to England quickly; but I didn't, I just couldn't – not yet. I knew I hadn't found the answers to my questions; all I was finding were more questions. I had many glimpses of what I knew were truths, but I didn't have the whole picture. It was like having several pieces of a puzzle, but with no idea of how they fit together. Not only were many puzzle pieces missing, so was the template showing where they should go. I had left England in emptiness and I refused to return until I knew how to fill myself.

Chapter 11

DARJEELING

In Darjeeling I visited yet another Tibetan Temple. I was encouraged by people I met to meet the Lama in charge. I remembered the lesson on the rooftop in the Himalayas, that the Tibetan teachings were not what I needed, but part of me was still hoping I could find refuge. One thing I knew for sure was my love for the Tibetan people.

The Lama received people one by one in his room, but when it was my turn to enter, I felt absolutely no warmth or welcome from him. It was the only time in my experiences with Tibetan people where I didn't feel something special and I knew I did not belong there. He gave me no encouragement or even kindness and I started to leave with a feeling of disappointment and emptiness. I turned to face him just as he was greeting someone else and before the door to his room shut I saw a radiant smile on his face, intended not for me, but for his new visitor. I knew I shared in the love that was radiated; he gave me his blessing even though it was not his intention. The blessing was wonderful!

The "hotel" I stayed in was the cheapest I could find. My parents had sent me a hundred dollars while I was in Katmandu, but money was tight. The bedroom, a large dormitory was filled with beds providing no privacy and no separation for men and women. There were just two of us staying that night, but I felt my own disorientation affected the young man who was my room companion.

He had been living on the fine line between sanity and insanity that many travelers walked and he crossed over. He was sobbing, completely out of control of his emotions, begging for help. I thought the connection to me, however tenuous, had done something to cause his imbalance; somehow my confusion had passed to him. He was taken to the local mental hospital, where hopefully he received the help he needed.

The silence fell like a stone. I was alone in the huge dormitory. Confusion, guilt and loneliness tried to overwhelm me and I prayed desperately. I blamed myself, I prayed, pouring with tears, begging God to take my life rather than allow me to cause harm to anyone else. Deeper into the night, as I lay in my narrow cot, there was a tremendous thunderstorm; I arose, standing next to the window. Lightening flashed all around. I again tearfully prayed, "Please," "Strike me with lightening rather than hurt some-one, make it impossible for me to harm another. *Please.*"

The thunderstorm raged and suddenly my whole body was filled with white light. I had no fear, feeling more alive than I had been for a long while. The guilt was gone. I was acutely aware of the power of God. My prayer had been answered directly.

Darjeeling was another place where loneliness and fear crept back in. I knew if I were to return to England, I would have to travel to Calcutta, yet I did not feel ready. The thought of being in Calcutta terrified me and I didn't meet anyone else who was travelling in that direction. I had no goal, other than trying to grow so I could reach the ideal I had seen in Mitzu. How to do that, I had no idea; where to go, I had no idea; what that even meant, I had no idea. England hadn't held any answers for me before, why should it now?

The day two Sikhs met me and offered me friendship, I was confused and lonely. I didn't see it was not friendship they wanted. These two men merely wanted my western body and one of them took what he wanted against my will.

The next day I left for Calcutta.

CALCUTTA

Calcutta was steeped and immersed in poverty, in filth. I had to agree with the name, "The Black Hole of Calcutta". Because of my British passport, I didn't have the worry of visas in India, I could stay indefinitely.

It was easy to find the area of cheap hotels for travelers as most people spoke English. My money almost depleted, I stayed in the cheapest place possible. It was definitely a step up from the lodgings in Darjeeling, but it was still a total dive. There were cubicles, a half-wall surrounding each bed affording little privacy. I remained in Calcutta, in the same hotel for almost five months. In contrast to the Himalayas, this was a living hell.

Alone, I wandered to the open market filled with stalls of fruit and vegetables, inevitably followed by an onslaught of beggar children holding out their hands. "Bakshish, bakshish" they called, "money, money". I learned quickly if you gave a little to one of the children, more would appear; they emerged as if from the ethers. There was nowhere I could go without attracting a following of ten to fifteen children. I had very little money, but to them I must have seemed so very rich.

There was an atmosphere of hopelessness in Calcutta; people lay side by side on some streets, many sleeping, some asking for money, some already passed from this life. I stepped over the prostrate bodies. Every so often, authorities would come and pick up the remains of those who hadn't survived the night. The worst were the little children, lying with their mothers who had prostituted themselves to survive. The inevitable result being another mouth to feed. Their eyes lifeless, the only future for them, to be a beggar themselves.

Monsoon season came, rains poured, drains filled and overflowed; everywhere was flooded by filthy water. I sloshed my way through the fetid streets that swam with garbage and raw sewage - sometimes up to my knees, occasionally higher. Near my hotel was a mountainous pile of garbage. Crows and beggars regularly competed for scraps only the most desperate could possibly find edible. On occasion, some-one would urinate on the pile and move on. The stench, compounded by the intense heat and humidity was horrendous. You could shower in Calcutta and before you stepped out and had time to dry you would again be drenched in sweat. The noise and activity was continuous.

After a few overwhelming days, I met a fellow traveler who persuaded me to go to an opium den with him. During my time in India and Nepal, I had not touched any drugs (though I had been offered many times), but this time, I was desperately in need of companionship and I stupidly went. Almost as soon as I arrived, before I had time to do more than take in the scene of sallow faces and haze, the police arrived. My "friends" ran off and left me to my fate.

I found myself in the back of a rickety police wagon with bars on the windows and a guard by the door. I was hemmed in by Chinese opium addicts being hauled to the police station. The siren wailed moving people out of the way. I was in a state of absolute dreadful disbelief. The opium made the Chinese a very yellow color; their appetites were also sated by the drug making them incredibly skinny, sickly and sallow.

Anyone thinking of using heavy drugs should have the opportunity of sitting in such a situation, surrounded by a particularly sad reality amid lives which had lost purpose. I was terrified, the ride seemed to take forever, but I would rather have lived that moment of terror than the absolute apathy I felt from my fellow prisoners.

Escorted into the police station I was left to wait in an oppressive, dark hallway. The Chinese prisoners had been led off elsewhere. Fears of being imprisoned in India were definitely on my mind, yet, when the policeman opened the door to his sunlit office and I was offered a cup of tea, I knew my reality was no where near as bad as the place my imagination had dumped me. The officer was fascinated by me. I was English, young, pretty and travelling by myself. Rather than threaten prosecution he did his best to charm me, making me promise to meet him for a date the following afternoon (a date which I never attended). I was set free a little wiser.

I had been in Calcutta a couple of weeks before I met a young Chinese man named Michael. Slightly older than me, he reminded me of Mitzu. But Michael turned out to be a very angry young man, bitter and resentful about having to live in India, (his parents had escaped from China). He felt there was nowhere for him to go and he had no hope; he felt trapped in Calcutta. He attached himself to me as he saw an opportunity to escape – I was a ticket to the West, though it took me some time to be conscious of his intentions. I was no-where near ready to board an airplane back to England, something vital still missing.

For a while I thought Michael would at least help with the loneliness. He showed me how to climb onto the roof of the hotel where I was staying giving me relief from the craziness and noise. He took me to a discotheque where I saw the other side of life in Calcutta; but it seemed strange and out of place, two different cultures colliding.

He also introduced me to a wonderful dessert - gulab jamun (sweet little balls of something indescribably delicious in sugary syrup).

I had the opportunity to distribute food to the poor, not with Mother Theresa, but with an English man whom Michael introduced me to. He fed the poor daily, riding around in his rickety van taking food to pick up points where people gratefully and desperately waited. It was a completely different view of Calcutta and it felt good to be with someone who was doing what he could to make a difference.

I still held tremendous conflict inside me. How to respond to such poverty? A part of me wanted to train to be a nurse and come back to help, but that part was from guilt, not love. I had not learned that *I* could do something to help *on my own* and I had not yet found compassion for another human being. I did not understand my own value therefore failed to see the true value of another.

Late one afternoon as I was walking alone, an elderly Indian beggar came to me, asking for money. He was so skinny I don't know how he was still standing, it was obvious he would not live for much longer and yet I refused to help. He stood there with his desperately thin arm outstretched for help, eyes pleading and I didn't give him anything. I had grown cold. I had seen so many beggars, I closed myself off from his suffering. When he left, his last hope drained away, I had to look at myself and I was disgusted.

I only had a few dollars left, but that was no excuse. I knew I could get more money if needed and I knew I could leave India and Calcutta behind whenever I wanted. I could no longer judge the rich people in India who were cut off from the daily reality around them, stepping over the dying on the street while wearing gold jewelry; dancing in the discotheque as if death were not just outside the door. I was no different.

Not everyone became desensitized; the English man always gave away food, every day, even if he was not feeling well. Mother Theresa never stopped giving and loving, continually inspiring others to do the same. We have choice - and at the time I cut off my heart instead of having compassion.

The elderly beggar haunted me and I have repented many times for my coldness. For numerous years I wouldn't leave even one mouthful of food on my plate even if I was not hungry. It was not until I visited China thirty years later that I felt completely forgiven, and knew I had finally grown my heart.

Chapter 13

PURI

My relationship with Michael deteriorated rapidly. His anger and frustration progressively magnified. His pent up rage reached a head and was no longer contained. He beat me, not badly, but enough to make it clear I needed to leave. The only way out was to return to England.

He realized he had gone too far, blowing his chance of leaving India with me and he became excessively possessive, not letting me out of his sight. I agreed to go on vacation with him to give us a chance to work things out and told him I would then return to England, sorting out the paper work for him to join me. I lied. Any trust in him had been violated, I merely tried to humor him until I could get away.

We visited Puri, a seaside town south of Calcutta. The beach was beautiful, a huge expanse of soft, fine sand edged with lush, tropical greenery, the water warm. There was enough familiarity that I found myself relaxing into how I always felt at the ocean; the simple joy of playing in the waves as they pulled at my toes, the horizon stretching forever, the gentle ebb and flow easing me back into harmony.

The Indian women modestly wore their saris into the water, and I followed their example. It seemed strange to wear so much covering and the sari clung to me. I discovered they held their moisture long after exiting the ocean, feeling wonderfully cool next to my body.

The next day we strolled the quiet streets. Puri held none of the intensity of Calcutta and Michael also mellowed but I was still trying to figure out how to get away from him.

I *knew* I had to go down a narrow lane, there was an absolute insistence in me. On the left side was a green, wooden doorway I was intensely drawn towards. There was a quality of absolute peace. Michael didn't want to enter, but I had no choice, I was completely compelled. As I passed through the door I could breathe deeply and freely again.

The atmosphere was calm, holy and encompassing. I felt safe. A haven from all the chaos I experienced. I found the strength to stand up to Michael, to be assertive and I insisted on staying. Nothing could have stopped me, certainly not a mere mortal. Michael returned to Calcutta.

The doorway led to an ashram where Swami Hariharananda Giri resided and taught. He had a wonderful face, somewhat hidden behind his magnificent long white beard. His luminous eyes filled with compassion as he took me in and allowed me to stay. During the week, I spent in his company, five days were in silence. Swami Hariharananda or Swamiji, as he was affectionately known, had spent over eleven years in silence and though it was a small token I felt I should remain without speech for at least a few days.

He lovingly placed his gifted hands on my head. The confusion attached to me sloughed off. I was amazed at how many irrelevant thoughts I had. My mind was finally cleansed. Pure light washed through me bringing clarity of thought. What a gift those days of silence were, my inner guidance becoming clearer.

During that short time, Swamiji taught me the meditation technique of Kriya yoga. He was incredibly kind, his eyes conveying a gentle spirit filled with love and goodness. He was a wise father-figure to me and I am grateful for his beautiful presence.

I have carried his advice in my heart for the rest of my life; he told me I should reach only for God, and not let gifts - even a gift for healing - distract me. "Aim always for God and let nothing separate you from that path", he taught.

The ashram was that of Sri Yukteshwar. Swamiji was a fellow disciple of Yogananda, the last living disciple of Sri Yukteshwar. Through Swami Hariharananda a relationship with the line of gurus, Babaji Maharaj, Lahiri Mahasaya, Sri Yukteshwar and Paramahansa Yogananda was established.

I left with renewed strength, connectedness and the tool of meditation. I was also armed with pictures of each guru to help my meditations. My heart was filled, given a new beginning.

I was finally ready to return to England; I had the tools and guidance I needed, knowing from now on my journey would lead only forwards.

Part Two

"You must not let your life run

the ordinary way;

Do something that nobody else has done,

something that will dazzle the world.

Show that God's creative principle

is in you."

Paramahansa Yogananda

MOVING FORWARD

ENGLAND

Early September, I arrived back in England as Falmouth Art College was beginning the fall semester. I had applied to this college before going to Plymouth, but didn't get accepted. The enrollment was already full, but I decided to approach them anyway, stating firmly I had just returned from India and had a lot to express.

I was accepted into the one year foundation course enabling me to gain exposure to various media before deciding on a major. Basically, I played with photography, sculpture, print making, drawing and painting. English education, at that time, was free and it was a wonderful opportunity.

I was grateful to be back in Cornwall and meditated every day. I felt in control of my life. I was older than most of the foundation students as they were straight out of high school, but there were a couple of people my age I connected with. We hung out a lot, talking and laughing, but still, before the foundation course was over, I began to feel restless. England was stifling me, there was nowhere to go and even though I had been accepted to a good art college; it was not what my heart and spirit called for.

Late May, as the Cornish coast was warming up to welcome the summer tourists, an American, Aaron, whom I met in Puri, wrote and invited me to come to America. He arranged for Swami Hariharananda to visit New York; it was Swamiji's first trip outside India and Aaron was excited to share his wisdom with the West. Aaron generously offered me food and lodging if I could get myself to America. I took him at his word, left England with fifty dollars in my pocket and a return ticket, one I would never use.

In June 1975 I left Cornwall for the last time, once again hitchhiking alone through England. My first couple of rides were nothing extraordinary, but then I was picked up by a middle aged man. He looked normal enough, fairly non-descript, and I was still naive enough to trust strangers. He told me he was a tree surgeon and needed to stop for a job which would take a half hour or so. He would then drive me many miles further. I was grateful to not stand by the road with my thumb out for a while, so I thought "what the heck," I would learn what a tree surgeon did for a living. It sounded interesting and I wasn't in a hurry.

I was in the woods, miles from anywhere, with a strange guy who had a blowtorch. All seemed fine, it was peaceful, the trees were in full leaf and I settled down to wait while he went to work. He described how he was helping the tree and he talked about different tree diseases; he seemed quite knowledgeable and appeared to like his work. I felt relaxed. Suddenly he turned the blow torch towards me. I backed up against the tree, a blow torch in my face as this man, who had seemed like a regular person, transformed into a rapist. Instead of being taken over by fear, I became completely still and present. I was held in a peaceful state by my line of gurus, Babaji, Lahiri Mahasaya, Sri Yukteshwar and Paramahansa Yogananda - they were all there, all with me, protecting me. I felt them physically and I actually saw their images, not just in my mind but standing beside me. I experienced an incredible calm. The tree surgeon was powerless. Putting out the blow torch, he wept, begging my forgiveness.

We left the woods; he gave me a ride to the first stopping point and bought me a cup of coffee. After we talked for a while, he agreed to get some help. I was more than a little nervous when I again put out my thumb, and was relieved when a young couple pulled over to offer me a ride. I was exhausted. I slept the rest of the journey.

I stayed in London for a couple of days, reconnecting with Alan, the owner of the head shop in Plymouth. It was gratifying and reassuring when he told me "You don't need me any more, you are on your way."

The ferry took me from the shores of England to Amsterdam where I stayed overnight in readiness for the next days flight to America.

Chapter 15

Chapter 16

AMERICA

As the plane took off from Amsterdam, the same feeling came over me as when I left for India. All fear and even anticipation was wiped away.

It was dusk as I landed in New York, the plane descending through a spectacular smoggy sunset. I felt something which I had not experienced before; the ugliness of Newark was irrelevant, it was the atmosphere that I sensed, one of hope. The sense of freedom was palpable. I wonder how many others have had this same feeling. I don't know how many Americans understand this gift. When you live in it day after day, it is easy to take it for granted.

No-one was at the airport to meet me; I expected to get a ride, but when I called Aaron, he said I should take a cab; my fifty dollars was not going to last long! The cab dropped me by an apartment building in the Bronx at ten o'clock at night. There was no sign of Aaron or Swamiji. I rang the doorbell, but no-one knew what I was talking about.

It was surreal and the scary stories I had heard of America began to pollute my mind. I soon discovered that the address where I now stood alone in the dark and the phone number were different. Luckily I discovered a phone booth, fumbled with my money, trying to figure out which coin was the right one in this new currency and was given the correct address. Emotionally bedraggled, I arrived at 1:00 am on June 21st in Manhattan.

It was different being with Swamiji in America, he was surrounded by so much activity, but his presence still carried the immense peace I remembered from Puri. I stayed with him the entire time he was in America, from New York to Washington, D.C.

In D.C. we stayed with a couple who had studied Kriya yoga under a disciple of Swamiji's. Luis was from Bogata, Columbia and Vicki, his wife was American; they had a beautiful, raven-haired four year old daughter, Christina.

Swamiji stayed for several days before returning to India, teaching us deeper levels of meditation; his kind, generous spirit affecting all who were around him. I was not sure what to do next; my ticket back to England was not for two months and I had virtually no money. Vicki and Luis generously let me stay with them for a while. My short term plan was to earn some money and venture to South America to study pottery, then on to Japan to continue my education of ceramics.

Fortunately, a young Hispanic guy, Juan, also part of the meditation group, was travelling to Canada. He invited me to go with him and since I had a British passport, I could work in Canada more easily than in America. I was glad I didn't have to put my thumb out alone, and he was grateful to have a young woman to travel with who was more likely to get rides!

We visited Quebec, connecting with a group of young people. They informed me it was almost tobacco picking season and the tobacco farmers were always looking for seasonal help. They invited me to stay with them until they left. Juan stayed in Montreal, but I went with my new-found friends to the countryside outside of Quebec City; we shared a simple house close to the forest.

Tobacco picking time was at hand, I traveled with my Canadian friends to London, Ontario. Many people were looking for work as it paid well and housing and food were provided as part of the deal. Some of the potential workers were rough looking but I was fortunate to find a job with a group of English students. Their jobs were pre-arranged, but there was room for one more.

Picking tobacco was horrible work, but the students were fun and I was accepted as one of them. We had two dorms, one for the girls and one for the guys, and even though we were tired at the end of the day, it felt good to socialize. The familiarity of English company was comfortable to me and I didn't feel shy. We ate all of our meals together in the farmhouse, good solid food served in huge quantities. I couldn't believe how hungry I got working outside all day.

My job was not actually to pick the tobacco - the guys did that - but I had to slap the newly picked leaves onto a conveyor belt. Bend down, grab a handful from the bin and place them on the conveyor belt, straighten them; bend down, grab another handful, place them on the conveyor belt, straighten them; bend down, grab a handful – over and over all day. I learned to look out for the huge, ugly green caterpillars and tried to shake them off the leaves without touching them. With that brief distraction I got behind and had to straighten the leaves more quickly and grab another handful as fast as possible.

Some mornings the dew was so cold my fingers ached and the beginnings of arthritis crept in. My fingers which had always been straight grew somewhat bent. But the money was worth it; by the end of the six week picking season I had accumulated $1,600.

My twenty-second birthday was spent on that Canadian tobacco farm. It was a stormy day, but the farmer expected us to continue working. The storm loomed closer and closer, slowly the lightening and thunder manifested. We needed to quit working *now*. I would take responsibility. Two minutes later, just as we backed away from the machine, the conveyor belt was struck by lightening. The farmer had nothing to say; he stood there stunned. I was once again grateful to be alive. That storm was a God send.

The growing season over, it was time to move on. I decided to head to Thunder Bay and then take a plane to Boulder, Colorado where my brother, Patrick, was living. Even though I had been warned never to hitchhike in the U.S. alone, I had heard no such warnings about Canada. I decided it was safe. It was obvious things were in harmony but I still took a deep breath before I put my thumb out once more. Hitchhiking is a great teacher of patience; a ride may appear instantly or it may take hours, but inevitably a ride always showed up and getting frustrated made no sense at all.

I had a known destination and that was a good feeling. My ride to Sudbury was straight forward and I easily found the address I had been given.

Sister Theresa was known locally as the "Singing Nun", she sang everywhere she went. When I first met her, she invited me into her office and asked if I would like some ale to drink. This struck me as being a rather unusual offer for a nun. I never had liked beer much anyway but it seemed impolite to refuse and I *was* thirsty. I became even more confused when she presented me with a glass of water. She looked at my befuddled expression, I'm sure it was just the one she had been hoping for, and with a huge, mischievous grin said, "Adam's Ale!" I had to like her instantly. She was delightful and not only gave me somewhere to sleep, but also kept me company through the day.

She took me on a walk around the rather ugly mining town; Sudbury with its profusion of slag heaps was about as charming as its name, but as we passed under a bridge, she suddenly burst into song. I was still at an age where I was easily embarrassed; yet she was entirely unselfconscious as her strong voice rang out, obviously experiencing absolute delight in how it echoed. Her joy was contagious, not just to me, but to the hearts of all who heard her. The ugly streets became brighter in her presence.

On our walk we discussed religion; I shared my belief in reincarnation. Her response was, "I'm sorry, but we only have one chance." There was something in the surety of her expression that made a dent in my beliefs. I decided whatever the truth, the only really important thing was to live life the best way possible. That way, if it is my last life - I did my best; if I was to be reborn - I did my best; and if this was my only life - I would still do my best.

That evening, she took me to the chapel with her as she offered her evening prayers. I was awkward at first as I was unfamiliar with churches but I closed my eyes and meditated. As I sat there, an image of Jesus came into my mind. One tear involuntarily came out of my eye and rolled down my cheek. This surprised me. I began to repent for always denying Jesus. It was the first time in my life I knew Jesus was real, even though Paramahansa Yogananda had talked about him in his book 'Autobiography of a Yogi'. My upbringing was so strong that it took a lot for the possibility to sink in.

My journey in Canada was blessed, my path and the signs along the path true; there was a very clear spirit around me. I was deeply grateful to the "Singing Nun" and to Canada as I left, hitchhiking on to Thunder Bay. It was a blissfully uneventful trip and I reached Colorado the next day.

Patrick, my brother, had chosen to live and go to a university in Boulder, so I spent a few days with him. He was at the university most of the time and it gave me a chance to gather my thoughts, to rest up in a more normal environment.

After a few days, I decided to return to Washington D.C. as Vicki and Luis had invited me. Since I decided I would travel south next, it seemed like the right place to start. It felt good to have money in my pocket and I easily found a ride to D.C. from the college notice board.

During the couple of months I had been in Canada, Luis had made changes in his own life - he had joined the Unification Church. He had seen a billboard by the Ginseng Tea House. On the billboard was a picture of Rev. Sun Myung Moon. He felt it call to him somehow so he visited the Tea House to request a copy of Rev. Moon's teachings: "The Divine Principle". Without any pressure from anyone, he was convinced of the validity and truth in those teachings and joined the Unification Church.

Luis was inspired by what he was learning and told me I should attend a workshop. I liked Luis, grateful for his giving me somewhere to stay, but quite frankly I had absolutely no intention of going to any workshop. It was simply I already had a direction that was working very well for me. I had worked hard to find that path, cleared out a great deal of confusion and had no desire to re-introduce complications into my life. My mind was clear; I knew from my experience in Canada how in harmony I was and how well the meditation worked - why would I possibly want to try anything else?

Luis informed me of his view that the amount I could grow in ten years of meditating could be achieved in ten months in the Unification Church. It was still not enough to persuade me to go, but I promised him I would meditate on it and I did.

Throughout the evening I was alone in their daughter's bedroom, (they had moved her in with them to sleep enabling me to have a quiet place of my own for the time I was there). I connected to the picture of Yogananda and told him, "Don't worry, I am not going to the workshop." But as I examined his face in the picture, he was crying. I was not sure what that meant so I asked, "Do you want me to go to the workshop?" The picture changed, he smiled. This sounds strange, but I had learned by this time this was truly a "real" experience, just as real as sitting face to face with someone.

I knew Yogananda wanted me to go to the workshop but I was still hesitant and I asked, "Please, please, please protect me, don't let me be confused." I knew how devastating spiritual confusion was and I did not want to experience it again.

Attendance was small, just me and one other girl. I meditated as I listened to the lectures, intrigued by what I heard. It was as if all the truths I figured out during my travels were confirmed, but there was also more, far more, that made sense. I frequently thought, "Of course, I should have known that."

During the second part of the lectures, the girl who was with me began to argue with the lecturer. My eyes filled with white light blinding me; and my ears were blocked out by sound, a ringing from inside, eliminating all other noise. I felt completely calm. As the lecturer took charge of the discussion again, my eyes and ears gradually cleared until I could see and hear clearly. I knew my prayer to the gurus had been answered, they were protecting me from any confusion.

In the "Parables of History" lecture that came towards the end of the workshop, everything pulled together; historical events I had learned from European history in school suddenly made sense. My head was reeling and the atmosphere was charged; I felt a spiritual "thickness" around me. The words I had been told in East Nepal came into my head and I said aloud, "I was told in East Nepal the Messiah would come and unveil the parables of the Bible; this is what I just heard, therefore Rev. Moon is the Messiah!" It was like an explosion - all the weight around me scattered. I laughed, I felt so free.

The truth of my understanding helped make sense of my life's journey so far; I could see how God had been leading me - out of atheism - to this realization. I *felt* the truth of it. I had found what I needed, what I had been looking for and I decided to stay in Washington D.C. as a member of the Unification Church – that's right, a Moonie!

UNIFICATION CHURCH

A couple of days after joining, I changed my name back to Deborah, my birth name; I had gone by the name Daisy since I was eleven years old. I also cut my hair short and gave up my hard earned tobacco money. This was the standard practice in the Unification Church and was designed to help you separate from the influences of this world - not always a bad thing. In many ways, I felt like a spiritual baby.

One girl was quite frankly ditzy, yet I saw how spiritually 'bright' she was and how innocent. It was an education being around her, me thinking I actually knew something and looking at her as if she were ignorant. I stayed up all night, praying for humility. Surely with this extra effort I would be humble by morning!!

A year or so later in Manhattan, I was with a couple of friends, Mathew and Ray who I liked very much; we would hang out together on the rare occasions when we were not too busy. One time, Bill, whom I previously knew from the meditation group, and who I introduced to the Unification Church, joined us. He told my friends I was lucky the Unification Church had taken me in, how I had been wandering aimlessly with no purpose and basically I was fortunate not to be on the streets. I felt beaten down, my pride in having made my trip to India and getting to America radically erased.

I maintained my connection to meditation when I first joined, but learned to pray as well. Several people from the meditation group joined the Unification Church, but there was one person, Paul, I specifically wanted to be a part of it. He had traveled with Swami Hariharinanda from

New York to Washington D.C. was dedicated and talented at meditation. He lived in Minneapolis and I decided to pay him a visit.

A tradition in the Unification Church is to take a gift when you visit someone. All I had was some fundraising product. I arrived in Minnesota with the gift of a box of Baby Ruth candy bars and the companionship of a Unification Church sister, Jenny, as I was not trusted to travel on my own. It was freezing; this was the end of November and it felt as if the water droplets in my breath were turning to ice inside my nostrils.

Paul greeted me warily; I am quite sure the box of twenty Baby Ruth candy bars didn't help, but he invited us in. We talked for a while; sometimes he connected to what I shared and sometimes he didn't. The sister who came with me just prayed. There was a short period where I became spiritually open and I was shown while praying for him, when we were connected his spirit became bright and beautiful. When he separated from me, however, I saw him become ugly and distorted. It saddened me as it became obvious he was not interested in Rev. Moon and it was time to leave, without him. I am not saying this was truly what was happening to his spirit, but it is what I needed to see.

I had very little relationship with Jesus, apart from my beautiful experience in the chapel in Canada. During a lecture titled "Mission of the Messiah", I became "open" again as I had been while visiting Paul. I was hanging on the cross, as Jesus had been, I was seeing through Jesus' eyes. It was similar to my experience with Paul, but in this case I was looking out over a huge mass of people. As the crowd connected to Jesus, they were spiritually beautiful; but as they drew away, they became extremely ugly, disfigured and grotesque.

I felt profound sadness, tears pouring from my eyes. I thought of Jesus' desperate prayer as he fell to the ground in the Garden of Gethsemane "Remove this cup from me; yet not what I will, but what thou wilt", a prayer which I knew had not been said in a moment of weakness, but a prayer of great strength and deep love. It was a prayer offered for the sake of all people even as they taunted and crucified him. I was shaken as I came back into myself, profoundly moved by the level of compassion I experienced.

I found the U.C. difficult; it was hard following a leader and doing whatever I was told; it was hard to go fund-raising, I didn't like selling candy door to door; it was hard to listen to lectures, being told one day I would also have to lecture. The experience helped me challenge many of my perceived limits, especially my shyness.

LEARNING TO LISTEN

It was about learning to listen to my true voice; learning to distinguish the differences. There were times when the truth was undeniable - starting with my car crash and then in the Himalayas when I knew God/Spirit. Eventually, I learned to trust my inner voice completely. If I am experiencing self-judgment, limitations, denial, my "listening" is incorrect.

I am certain inner knowing is available to each one of us, though it may be perceived in different ways. To me it was a voice and often a physical sensation of rightness, chills if you will and occasionally (as in the experience with Jesus) visual. To hear the voice correctly took practice; it was not a voice in my mind so much as a voice in my heart and I needed to develop the ability to listen in my heart and not my head.

Rev. Moon was the first one who taught me where to listen in a concrete way; he described it as being a place where the vertical line going through your body (being your connection to God) met a horizontal line coming through your heart (being your interaction with the world). That is the point from where you listen, where God and the world are in harmony; living from there is the goal.

Simple, not easy.

Two people especially moved me with their wisdom. Both were older members; Philip B. and Lady Dr. Kim, who was a medical doctor and also a Korean Shaman. The church was full of enthusiastic members, but they were mostly young and I needed someone with more spiritual experience to guide me. Both Philip and Lady Dr. Kim had walked a different path than most Unification Church members. What impressed me most about Phillip B. was he had undergone his own personal persecution.' I did not get the sense he felt he was "older" or "better", he talked to me like a regular person.

There was a definite hierarchy in the Unification Church coming both from the basic teachings and from the Korean culture.

I was not in D.C. for long before I knew it was time to leave. I had worked on the Washington Monument campaign, a huge event that we witnessed for, tirelessly. We slept very little, the momentum kept us going. However, once over there was a distinct lack of direction. After a while it was imperative for me to go elsewhere. Fortunately I was sent to upstate New York, to the seminary. I was permitted to go with the understanding this would be a short visit, but I knew I would not be returning to Washington.

At the seminary I helped with the 21 day workshops and became assistant to Rev. Sudo. He was another 'older' member who was absolutely wonderful. Japanese, his height about 5' 2". He looked after me as if I were family; he had a wife and little daughter, but as was common in the church he was separated from his family for long periods of time.

The seminary gave me the opportunity to spend time alone. Completely giving myself to God in prayer, I asked to speak for God, to live for God, that my whole life be for Him. Nothing would stop me from being with God. I was absolutely single focused.

The Church standard regarding marriage mandated three years (sometimes as long as seven years) of dedicated, celibate life after which a mate would be chosen for you by Rev. Moon in a "matching" ceremony. This led to sometime later being blessed as husband and wife. You needed at least three spiritual "children", (people you introduced to the U.C.) to qualify. You had to fast seven days, drinking only water. Other conditions consisted of fund-raising and witnessing. This was a serious commitment.

The peaceful atmosphere of the seminary was a wonderful opportunity to connect with nature. We went fishing in the Hudson River. A net was placed in the river as the tide went out, trapping the fish in the shallow water and then we waded out in mud up to our knees, water soaking up to our thighs. Slogging through the mud was tough going and every so often a fish would brush my legs. I caught about ten carp with my hands, some bright orange and some lighter in color.

Of course, this was the Unification Church. The Church was all about duty and mission, responsibility for your ancestors and the sorrow in God's heart which we needed to relieve. Catching fish was a serious prayer.

Rev. Moon spoke for hours and hours. He often talked about true love, how we must learn to love all different types of people; how we must break down all barriers, so when we go to Spirit World, we will have no limits.

He taught the Messiah is a mediator, one who comes as a sinless human being between God and man. But he also taught that we should all be messiahs. Everyone on earth having the potential to become one with God – it is our "true" destiny. There was one talk which inspired me greatly. He spoke of giving love injections to God, to surprise God by doing something unexpected.

Rev. Moon's life was a major part of the U.C. teachings. We were taught of his sacrifices, especially during his experiences in prison camp in North Korea, where he was beaten and left for dead. The concept of sacrifice and suffering permeated the Unification Church. Joy for the simple sake of joy and fun were not part of it.

Mr. Sudo once told me I had a raisin heart; he said my heart was small like a shriveled, dried raisin. Even though this hurt, I felt some truth in his statement and it made me pray more to learn how to love, to love unconditionally, to love with God's heart; to feel compassion without judgment.

Not long after this, Rev. Moon issued new directions; groups were sent out witnessing around the country to bring more members. Mr. Sudo was in charge of a team being sent to Ohio and I went with him. The members of Mr. Sudo's team were given different assignments; fund-raising, cooking, team leader etc. He didn't give me an assignment and when I asked him, he prayed and then said, "Your mission is to bring together physical and spiritual world." This resonated in me, even though I had no idea what it meant and no idea how.

As I was witnessing, I met a young black man whom I believed to be spiritually clear. He talked about joy, living in God's joy. Chapter one of the Divine Principle (Rev. Moon's teaching) begins by expressing the thought that we are all seeking happiness, but the daily reality was one of a level of sacrifice that was virtually impossible to attain and there was a great deal of judgment; you could never be good enough.

I appreciated this friend who viewed life more joyfully. I told Rev. Sudo about him and how I was considering learning more from him. Rev. Sudo slapped me. His action completely surprised both if us. He was genuinely frightened for me.

Where had I been listening when I was thinking of leaving? It had sounded so good. Had it been what God wanted? Had I been deceived as Rev. Sudo thought? I still wasn't sure; but I trusted Rev. Sudo's heart towards me - that was clear - so it was there I put my trust. I decided to stay with the Unification Church.

New orders came sending our team to New York. Another huge event, this one at Yankee Stadium, was being planned. There was also a new venture; a newspaper was being published. Witnessing was paramount.

Due to lack of sleep and food with little nutrition, it was hard to stay awake even when talking to people. When I sat down, I could barely keep my eyes open but we were told to connect to a certain number of people a day, so there was no stopping.

After a couple of weeks of this I heard a voice telling me to get on the train to Newark, New Jersey; there was someone for me to meet. I did so, but as I looked around the train station I was acutely aware there was no-one; it had simply been a waste of time and effort. It made me more aware of striving to listen correctly which is hard to do when exhausted.

I told Mr. Sudo and he gave me ginseng tea (usually reserved for the older members,) and made sure I ate meat - to ground myself. He also allowed me to sleep more. Before this I had been in strategy meetings which started at about 11:00 p.m. and sometimes lasted until 1:00 or 2:00 a.m. and still had to get up at 5:00 or 5:30. It felt blissful to actually lie down for a nap without guilt! I was probably the only Moonie ordered to sleep more not less; sleep deprivation was part of the example set by Rev. Moon. Rev Moon talked about becoming a perfect person, about mind/body unity, not harmony of mind and body but more about the mind overcoming the body's needs.

While in New York, I received a letter from Diane, whom I had befriended in the Himalayas. She told me

Mitzu was visiting his sister in New York City. Of course, I had to see him; he was still the reason why I strived so hard to find truth. Through this whole time, I remembered his peaceful presence. He continued to be my inspiration to grow spiritually.

I was delighted to see him, but as I tried to share with him, I realized there was nothing there; I no longer felt connected to him. He told me how he was searching and was traveling from hot spring to hot spring around the world. I said, "Surely the purpose of searching is to find something." But he didn't see it that way. I was nevertheless grateful to have this chance to be with him. Our paths had separated. I needed to be clear on this before I could move on and he had come to New York! I love the mathematics of how things work.

NEW DIRECTION

O nce the campaign concluded I settled into more of a routine. I began working at the church headquarters at West 43rd St., N.Y. Life was simpler and though there was still not a lot of sleep; at least, it was regular.

There was great anticipation about the upcoming matching and blessing ceremony. I understood the value of purifying myself. In fact this was one of the most treasured gifts I gained in the U.C. - how to purify the love relationship and let God into the deepest, most intimate parts of myself. I didn't look at the brothers as potential mates. In fact, I found most of them nerdy and unattractive.

I was still aware of my prayer in the chapel at the seminary, and I didn't even know if the Blessing was something in my future or not. The only way I played with the possibility was to examine my motives. The matching was out of your control; you did theoretically have three days to agree or disagree with Rev. Moon's choice, but there was great stigma attached to not trusting him, so I doubt many people said no.

Then Eric appeared, right when I was not looking, thinking or wanting, right when I was focused; resigned to being celibate for another several years, or possibly the rest of my life.

We all took life pretty seriously then. Hearing Eric's laugh echoing down the curving marble staircase lifted my spirits. Sometimes I heard his distinctive voice.

I was working reception and Eric was working in general building maintenance. He was too good looking, something I would deny myself to be enticed by; but something was "right". We found a little coffee shop in Manhattan; we had no money, so we would make one coffee last a long time, but no-one seemed to mind. We talked, occasionally out loud, but mostly from our minds; we had long conversations with each other without ever verbalizing a word.

What convinced me that something was supposed to happen between us occurred when he told me he had looked at me, seeing me as an old woman - with all the wisdom I would acquire shown in a multitude of age lines. Eric promised, literally, to take me into the pits of hell and he did this extremely well. But isn't that what I had asked for in my prayers at the seminary? I understood that God was in the pits of hell and that is where I wanted to be.

Eric took me, and several others to meet with Lady Doctor Kim. He felt the importance of the "mission" he needed to do and he knew it entailed being with a partner. When we met with Lady Dr. Kim, she asked me how many spiritual children I had; I answered three and she smiled. This was the number needed for the blessing. She talked to us about the family bed, having your children sleep in the bed with you, how it was such a gift of stability for your children; then she smiled again and we left.

I was beginning to see where this new direction was leading but I was not persuaded easily, I told Eric I needed to do two things first; to go to Belvedere Estate to pray at the Holy Rock and to do a seven day fast.

We went together to Belvedere, Rev. Moon's property in New York State. The property is guarded and you can only get in on a Sunday, but I knew George, the brother in charge of security. He happened to be at the front gate that day, he knew me well and trusted me when I said I *needed* to be there. We were granted entry and walked over to the Holy Rock to pray.

God came to me as clearly as He had done in the Himalayas and He asked me three times if I was ready to take this mission. He questioned whether or not I was ready and each time I said "Yes" I am ready. There was intense pressure and I had to be absolutely sure in my heart to be able to say yes, but after the third time, the pressure lifted and I felt huge joy. One thing I was clearly told was I had to trust Eric; it was also made clear that this would not always be easy.

After our prayers, we walked together across the manicured grounds to a small Asian bridge which spanned a narrow stream. We stood there together hand in hand, both knowing we received the blessing in that moment, not from Rev. Moon, but from God.

I knew if I was to deny the uniting of Eric and myself, I would have to deny everything I knew of Spirit. I would have to revert to being atheist, as this all came from the same place - the part of my heart that spoke so loudly, the part of my heart that *knew*. It was not from my mind, but from a much deeper place. From the same place I *knew* God in the Himalayas. A place undeniable.

Before I would agree to be with Eric physically I needed to do a seven day fast. This was a requirement for the blessing and the commitment was important to me. I had previously done several three day fasts, but as I am not large in physical stature, this was a huge undertaking. During the fast you drank only water and by the sixth day I was completely exhausted, I was down to 95 pounds, and had no energy, but I was spiritually clear.

I had a vision; I saw two children born in the dark, each one full of light individually but surrounded by darkness. I then climbed up steep golden stairs, often stumbling on my way. Two more children were born on the stairway. At the top of the stairs was a huge chasm and on the other side, at the same level, were Rev. and Mrs.

Moon. I felt sad as I saw they were so far away but the instant this thought came, a golden bridge spanned the gap between us and we began to cross over. Two more children were born on the bridge and as we greeted Rev. and Mrs. Moon in joy, one more child was born. Even though it was I who received the vision, both Eric and I knew we would have seven children.

This whole occurrence (other than the fasting) went entirely against the teaching of the Unification Church; there was no way to become a couple other than to be matched and blessed by Rev. Moon. I knew how much Mr. Sudo cared for me, I was quite sure he would understand and support me. I was wrong! He was devastated and thought I was making the hugest mistake of my life. He told me to meet with the group of leaders at 43rd Street. I agreed and faced the "council of twelve", twelve of the top leaders of the Unification Church, all of whom thought I was being tempted by Satan. As they questioned me, I became more certain of what I was about to do, no doubt existed. Even though I knew how much it hurt Mr. Sudo, this was what I needed to do, it was imperative.

After the meeting, I bounced down the stairs to where Eric was waiting for me in the lobby; he had been worried, afraid I would not be strong enough and he looked up at me almost in surprise as I said simply, "Okay, let's go!"

TOGETHER

We left with no money and no-where to go, but outside the church headquarters we met a Hispanic brother, Victor. We explained why we had to leave and he invited us to stay at his apartment with his aunt in Bedford-Stuyvesant, Brooklyn. He even gave us bus money to get there.

We spent our 'honeymoon' in the most run down, depressed area of Brooklyn; where the few stores that were not boarded up had heavy bars on the windows. We gathered pennies we found in a penny jar and bought a pot roast, which was immediately spoiled by a flood of roaches jumping into it. Our laughter surprised us. Even when Eric took my flute to pawn for food it seemed okay, but it stung when I found out it had only fetched $40.00.

Two weeks later we took a greyhound bus to Idaho, where Eric's parents lived. The Church paid for two tickets since we had been forced to leave. I was sick on the bus ride, barely maintaining over the several days across country. I was pregnant with our first child. I had known his conception; it was something exquisite when he was conceived. I 'saw' the cells multiplying inside, one then two then four, eight, until there was a mass, the beginning of new life.

We rented a tiny duplex in the North of Boise which had one small bedroom and a kitchen/living room. It was perfect for us. I had a strong yearning for a cat; for some reason I wanted a long-haired grey cat, my nurturing instincts were getting stronger as my belly enlarged. I loved cats having grown up with them, but we were not allowed to have pets in our little rental house.

It was a friendly neighborhood with quite a few kids around and Halloween brought a lot of activity. Three young kids came to the door, dressed in Star Wars costumes. As they turned to leave, I looked down to see a little kitten by my feet. I asked the kids if it was their cat, but they said no. I was delighted as I picked up the little fluffy grey ball and snuggled it.

You have to wonder why it was a long haired gray cat I visualized. Was it because that was what I wanted or because a grey cat was what was coming and so that particular image came to my mind? Or maybe I don't have to think so much, just accept Spirit was working. At the time, I was simply happy and knew he belonged with me. Several times the land lady came to the house, but she never saw Monsei, as we called him. I was talking to her on the porch with the door open, he was sitting right by her feet, but she didn't even notice!

We had virtually no money; our first Christmas was sparse though Eric's mother had sent us a few decorations which we hung on a house plant. I was almost seven months pregnant and there had been many times when we had only brown rice to eat. This first Christmas we had oatmeal in the cupboard, nothing else, but it was enough. Neither of us felt a need for more; for either presents or food.

We called it our 'Oatmeal Christmas' and thought about Jesus born in a stable with nothing. We ate simply and gratefully. I have never before or since felt the spirit of Christmas as strongly as that year. Late that afternoon, neighbors came over with a basket of fruit. A short while later, friends of Eric's parents brought a meat and cheese plate! No-one knew we had no money for food; yet, here we were surrounded by a feast! I sometimes tell the story of that Christmas to my children as they are surrounded by presents and goodies, thinking the trappings are a necessary part of the Christmas experience.

Our first son, David, was born in Idaho, away from the support of brothers and sisters in the church and away from the support of my own physical family. My parents visited from England for the birth, but he was three weeks late and they had already gone by the time he was born. The night before our son's birth, Eric had a dream of a stag standing on the top of a hill and knew it was a boy.

It surprised me how painful the birth was; I thought after my bout with dysentery in Afghanistan this would be no big deal. Wrong. But it was wonderful too. Soon after he arrived, I turned to Eric, exclaiming, "Let's do this again!"

Soon after we arrived home from the hospital doubts began to creep in, doubts about our course together and whether it was right to have this little son. The moment the thoughts began to formulate in my mind, I felt a presence answer me - "If you don't want me, then I don't want to be here." I knew it came from my baby. I felt dreadful and was shaken out of my disharmony. I regretted feeling I didn't want my child, even for a moment.

We had no money, I made paper mobiles for him, and as he grew he played in nature with pine cones and rose petals. We would walk together and watch sunsets.

It was in New Orleans, two and a half years later that our second son was born. Galen had been conceived the day after Christmas, in my mind consciously conceived for Jesus. He was born at the end of September in the heat and humidity of the South. We had no money for medical care. I didn't see a doctor until late in the pregnancy, so when I went into labor, we went to Charity Hospital. A pint of blood taken from my husband as payment.

Eric was not allowed in the labor room. I had to go through the entire labor on my own. Well, not entirely alone. There was a large, black nurse who yelled at me as I adjusted my position to ease the labor, "Get off your hands and knees" she yelled, "You're going into labor faster".

There was not much to look at in the very plainly painted hospital room; it reminded me of rooms I slept in while traveling, several beds laid out dormitory style with no extras. I had been taught in the birthing classes from my first son to find a focal point in order to keep your attention away from the pain. I doubt if anyone has ever stared quite so appreciatively at a light switch for hours!

Finally I yelled, "The baby is coming!" And my 'delightful' nurse said, "There are people here before you, you'll have to wait". "This baby is coming *now*," I screamed. She got the message, loaded me onto a cart, pushing me down to the delivery room. Believe me it is *not* comfortable being moved from a bed to a rolling cart with a baby's head emerging! Besides, I lost my light switch; my point of focus was gone!

The nurses were running, pushing me on the cart, others retrieved Eric sending him charging down the hallway putting on his medical gown. We met in the delivery room, Galen's head crowning, and in a minute or so he was born. The room became quiet, the delivery nurse burst into tears at this child who was so wanted. A wonderful Jamaican doctor, Dr. Benet, insisted on giving us bonding time.

Precious bonding time with a newborn was unheard of in Charity hospital. The babies were usually whisked away, taken to the nursery before any sexually transmitted disease could occur. The new mothers were laid out like cattle in a row, all waiting to urinate. Paint was peeling off the walls and a faucet was drip, drip, dripping to encourage us. After peeing, we were sent to the hospital ward.

I stayed in the dormitory room for as short a time as possible as I wanted to be with my son, leaving the hospital less than six hours after he was born. The daylight was refreshing; the first person we met on the steps outside the hospital was a fund raiser for the Unification Church selling red roses!

Chapter 21

RETURN TO NEW YORK

Galen was twenty-one days old, David two and a half when we returned to New York at the invitation of Lady Dr. Kim. Eric had been in touch with her by telephone, and she told us it was time to come back. We arrived at the New York airport with one suitcase and two children, not even a quarter for a telephone call. Fortunately, Lady Dr. Kim's assistant, Jeremy was there to meet us.

Lady Doctor Kim was a remarkable woman, one of the kindest, wisest people I have ever had the privilege of meeting. Eric's connection with her was stronger than mine. There was a mutual respect coupled with an understanding of his life's course. She was Eric's mentor.

Being in her presence was somewhat intimidating; she could really see you, intuitively knowing what was taking place. She saw the spirit world around you enabling her to have a unique perspective to your problems. She detected the cause then gave you a "condition" or action plan to eradicate it (cold showers, prayer or fasting). Her prayer, being of the highest, had already made sure that the negative influence would disappear, but the course of action was definitely up to the individual to complete. She once described her life as similar to tightrope walking - she needed to be so very careful in everything she did.

In my case, she advised cold showers. I was okay with fasting and prayer but cold showers - oh man! I really didn't like cold showers. I was asked to do a ten day condition of a long cold shower, twenty-one minutes. This seemingly negative influence that was being removed resisted greatly. The first day I procrastinated and procrastinated. I knew once I got out of bed I would have to get in the shower. Honestly, it took me until 4:00 pm before I could make myself move.

Gradually as the days of freezing showers past, I began to clear. Lower level spirits do not like discomfort; they want to be living the good life. I began to love and appreciate those cold showers and when the ten days was over, I felt cleansed.

The value of these types of "conditions" was enormous and I learned to take them very seriously. If I made a commitment to pray for forty days, then I did just that, if I made a commitment to fasting or cold showers then I did them. I also learned to set my own courses of action - not just to do what I was advised.

Lady Dr. Kim presided over many conditions for the Church. One ceremony focused on protecting Rev. Moon's life at the Washington Monument rally. There were rumors regarding how she had moved an earthquake from one part of the world (which was providentially important) to another part of the world where less people would be affected. Fact or fiction, there was a mystique about her which I had personally experienced, enough so that the earthquake thing was not out of the question. Knowing we were going to stay with her brought up a whole gamut of emotions ranging from a healthy respect to trepidation.

Probably in her mid-sixties at the time, Lady Dr. Kim was older than most of the members in America. She had been one of the earliest members to join in Korea. Not only was she a medicine woman in the non-traditional sense; she was also a medical doctor, delivering the first two of Rev. and Mrs. Moon's children. She told us of her anguish when one of those babies died shortly after childbirth. I was struck by her depth of heart as she shared very personal stories with us. She told of how she escaped over the mountains from North Korea with her young son who was only four years old at the time.

When I first arrived, she had looked at me and noticed dark spots of pigmentation on my skin, which she knew were from exhaustion. I had pushed far more than I should after Galen's birth and she told me to rest as much as possible. This I did, but I also stayed in the room with my children because of the old "I'm not worthy" thing.

During my stay, Mrs. Oh, one of the first members ever to join Rev. Moon, came to visit. This was of great significance in the Unification Church. I loved this lady. She was elderly and was not feeling well during her visit, I was worried about her and sat up with her all night. I put David to sleep keeping Galen with me. I stayed with Mrs. Oh, praying for her until she woke up the next morning. On waking, she looked at me in surprise. "Were you here all night?" she asked. I just nodded.

Later that day as I was back in the bedroom, I felt the presence of both Mrs. Oh and Lady Dr. Kim with me. They were testing my internal strength and I was aware of a great pressure in my head. "Let's see how much she can handle" were the words I heard as the pressure intensified. I stayed with it, not breaking, until I felt them say "O.K." Suddenly the intensity lifted, I had passed and I knew it was important.

I learned a great deal from Lady Dr. Kim. In the three months we lived there, she shared her wealth of knowledge about child-raising. She herself had five children and several grandchildren. In the Korean culture the young people listened to their elders and learned from them and had done so for generations.

There was one time when Galen was crying and she advised me to leave him alone to work it out. She had been right in this before; I used to pick up my children at the slightest murmur, which was not healthy on several levels. But this time, he needed me, I could feel it and I ignored her and went to my son. She looked at me with respect acknowledging that she, too, still had things to learn.

She shared more than just technical cooking skills with me; she showed me how to cook with the right energy and prayer. She taught me how to give energy to houseplants, not to the leaves, but into the soil where the plants received their nutrition and she taught me how to clean a chopping board not by seeing the dirt, but by looking deeper at the echo of the germs. She talked about Atlantis, not as a mythical place, but as somewhere she physically knew.

She insisted Eric get a job, or perhaps two jobs. She taught him the Korean standard towards work and scolded him for having such resentment of his parents, making him write a loving letter, thanking them for who they were. She advised me to start watching other children in my home; Galen was still only about three months old, but she said it was experience I would use later. The possibility also came up that we would have a baby for a different couple; this was not unheard of in the Unification Church.

In one day Eric found two jobs. They were humble jobs - one as an elevator starter, opening the elevator door for people as they headed to work; the other was sales in Sears. Two weeks later, after a two month stay with Lady Dr. Kim, we moved into an apartment in White Plains. It was December 15th - our third anniversary of marriage.

Eric's jobs changed and developed while my heart grew by taking care of lots of children including the births of two more sons. Stephen was born two and a half years after Galen, diving out with his arm first and never waiting for the doctor! And then Quinn came almost exactly three years after.

We had been attending the local Unification Church in White Plains, N.Y., tithing regularly. I occasionally had the chance to hear Rev. Moon talk in Belvedere, not far from our house. There were several sermons where I was in either the first or second row. It was different being that close to Rev. Moon and I opened my heart as honestly as possible, baring myself to his scrutiny.

A wonderful talk regarding "Inyong" (the Korean word for destiny) profoundly moved me. Speaking only Korean, all talks were translated into English as he spoke. He expressed the concept that even when we rub elbows with a stranger in the supermarket it has a meaning.

He shared the story of how one Korean woman was disturbed by a crazy guy yelling in the street in Seoul, but her attitude was not "Oh, let me run the other way", it was to look deeper and ask "Why?" As she looked around, she had seen her son, who had been separated from her since the Korean War when so many families had been split up. Rev. Moon told this story to teach us to see beyond the obvious, things do not happen merely by chance. If there was a car crash, you should look at possibilities, expanding your viewpoint.

He talked about how there had sometimes been thousands of years of preparation in what looked like a chance meeting and how all kinds of events had happened in the lives of our ancestors to create the opportunities that are presented to us now. That talk on "Inyong" struck me to my core, causing me to scrutinize every event in my life. It enabled me to look beyond the obvious situation at hand and to examine what was happening from a different, larger perspective.

Early in 1989, Oliver, who lived at the Church center in White Plains came to Eric and me saying our marriage should be blessed by Rev. Moon. In the Unification Church a blessing for previously married couples was being planned. This invitation surprised both of us. He arranged for an interview with Dr. Mose Durst, which I guess we must have passed, because soon we were preparing for the blessing. We went to New York City where we went to see Lady Dr. Kim; she procured the rings and took us to get matching gowns. She was happy but gave us important guidance, telling us no matter how intense it got we should not back out.

On April 7th 1989 there were over 140 previously married couples lined up in the room. Rev. Moon came in and we all bowed. He then talked. After a while, he became very angry; he saw a couple who had asked for permission to be blessed to each other previously and had been refused. They thought perhaps this was their chance, but when he saw them he was livid. He noticed another couple, and though he was rather more apologetic he told them they, too, had to leave. Several couples got up and left; the atmosphere could be cut with a knife and I was seriously wondering if we belonged there.

Sensing my doubt, Eric told me to be quiet and should we be questioned to let him do the talking. Sure enough a few minutes later an older Korean brother came over and asked if we had been directly under a leader and back in the church for seven years. Even though Eric confidently said "Yes", I doubted this was true. While internally conflicted, I united with him, keeping my mouth shut. Gradually as the tension cleared, Eric turned to me and answered my questioning look. "Lady Dr. Kim," he whispered, "for ten years". I realized he was right; we had, indeed, been under her direction for ten years, seven since we returned to New York. It was under her direction I babysat and Eric was working; we met the necessary conditions; it may not be witnessing or fund-raising, but we were doing what we were directed to do. In the end, there were 138 previously married couples left in the room for the Blessing. The ceremony was beautiful; there was a complete energy shift from the earlier intensity. I felt peaceful, in harmony with Eric as we exchanged rings.

Another part of the Blessing was the "indemnity stick" ceremony, which involved both husband and wife. Each person had to hit the other on the butt - hard - with a stick (actually a piece of two by four). The purpose was to resolve resentments of the past, from misuse of the sexual relationship; this was also supposedly the last and only time we would ever hit each other. The same ceremony was held for all couples getting blessed, previously married or not and technically I could see it was a good idea. But as we were called up to the stage I was still nervous. I had already seen tears and heard a few rather loud yells.

Eric was first, he bent over and I was told to hit him, to whack him as hard as I could. I tried, but I was not particularly strong and my efforts were not deemed good enough by the brothers watching, so they helped me, holding the stick with me as I hit Eric again, three times in all. Eric groaned. By my turn I had an idea of how hard I was about to get whacked. I didn't make a sound or even flinch and when I stood up the elder brother observing said emphatically, "*Strong* sister." I felt good - it was done.

As I left the stage I turned to see Mr. Sudo. He was beaming at me, *so* happy to see me, totally delighted I was there. He apologized for not understanding on that day over ten years before, when I tried to tell him I knew this was what God wanted. I reminded him he had once told me I had a shriveled raisin heart. I asked him if this was still the case and he said, "No, it is now a big squishy tomato!"

We returned to White Plains where we began a four month separation period, during which we were not to have sexual relations.

After the blessing and separation, when we made love, there was a difference; there was more clarity and purity. I hadn't realized it was not like that before, but there was a definite shift in the sacredness of our love-making - the connection with God directly present.

We consciously created our fifth child. Our daughter Kim was born in 1990. We had a midwife for my care, but this was New York and home deliveries were deemed illegal. She was over three weeks late and just as I thought I was finally in labor, it suddenly stopped. I was already at the hospital, but no contractions! We paced up and down the hallways for what seemed like hours. Eric found a sign which the janitors had left saying "slippery when wet!" and he carried it with us for a while in case my water broke; it was good to laugh and relax.

Eventually the labor kicked in and when she finally arrived, the nurses were delighted and echoes of "it's a girl!" resounded down the hall. I didn't realize how much it would mean to me to have a daughter, I loved my sons, but when Kim came into my life, I realized part of me had been lonely, there was a feminine part of me that had not been nurtured with all the male energy.

Babysitting became harder for me; I longed to be able to give my time to my own children. Lady Dr. Kim taught me to put other children first and I always did. I was taking care of a Chinese baby, my own daughter along with four older children. If both the babies needed me at the same time I would pick up the other baby first, before my own, as I knew my own children were secure and would be comforted merely by my voice until I could get to them, but it got harder on my heart. I loved babysitting until that last year - I had burned out.

Rev. Moon asked all members to go back to their home towns and work there. The high rent was getting impossible to keep up with and for the first time we were accumulating a credit card debt. We lived by an elementary school and even though it was a good school; people would hang out in the evenings. There were crack vials in the playground and graffiti on the play equipment and one day we received a warning from the school about an attempted kidnapping right off the school steps.

Eric went out late one night to take the garbage when a homeless guy jumped out of the bush. He was harmless, but it scared Eric and we thought how the kids would have reacted if it happened to one of them. David's bike that he paid for himself was stolen; I was tired of worrying about my kids. It was time to move.

Chapter 21

Chapter 22

IDAHO

Idaho here we come. Eric's Dad and sister lived there. It was where Eric graduated from high school and where David, our eldest son, had been born. We again had no money and no job, but this time we had a moving truck, five children and credit card debt.

The last forty miles into Boise was horrendous; I was driving the car with the children, Eric driving the truck with our belongings. But he became sick and was having to stop every few minutes. Idaho was a tough journey from beginning to end!

Eric soon found a job. Having trained in the mental health field and having worked at the Cornell Medical Center in White Plains, he had good qualifications which made finding work easier. He worked in a treatment center helping adolescents.

There had been a time in New York when Eric had been addicted to crack. He had always been attracted to drugs and every so often I would find him smoking marijuana, sometimes he used drugs that were harder. He hid things from me and when I questioned him, he said he needed to do it for God. He told me he had to go into difficult situations and turn them around. He said I wouldn't understand, telling me to trust him. At the prayer rock when Eric and I first got together I had been told it was important for me to trust Eric. But was he committed to a true path or lying to me and worse to himself?

Where did I start to lose my own knowingness? When did I start to put my trust in him more than in what I intuitively felt? When did I, as a woman, get lost? - living

119

for my children and my husband, putting everyone else first. I started turning to Eric, saying "What does God say?" instead of trusting my own inner voice.

If I were talking to someone with Eric there, from the corner of my eye I would see him subtly shake his head at me as if I had said something stupid. I had always been my own worst critic. In my earlier years I constantly scrutinized myself, now it was compounded by Eric.

I dreaded the thought of baby sitting in Idaho; it only paid about $1.00 an hour and I knew how much work it was. I had burned out - I just couldn't do it any more. I really wanted to raise at least one child without having to take care of other little ones. Eric got another part time job giving us enough money without my having to work for a while.

I volunteered at the school, teaching art classes to the kids. During this time art came back to me, a friend down the road asked me if I wanted to take calligraphy classes with her. The classes were offered for free by a Japanese man from Hawaii, on condition that I teach calligraphy to three other people; he loved the art, wanting to share it and preserve it.

"Free" I could do, but I still had to buy the materials. It was then I realized Eric resented my doing something for myself. The calligraphy was a huge gift; it calmed me and took me out of my self-critical brain. I practiced every day, loving it.

When I was six months pregnant, Eric was in a car crash. He was applying for a job and prayed about whether it was the right timing to put in an application. He felt, yes, it was. A short while later a white Cadillac ran a red light side-swiping him. It was clearly not his fault but he was hurt. The injury steadily worsened and the pain increased.

He kept working, but he had more and more difficulty moving his neck.

I was grateful for the calligraphy, I know how important your attitude is to a growing fetus and I tried to remain calm internally. I sang songs to all my children in the womb but this child loved Mozart piano concertos and I would play Mozart, practice calligraphy and for a while be at peace. Often when I drove Eric to work I would cry all the way home for him, but if I got too upset I felt pain in my womb and I knew I had to stay calmer. This little son was a teacher for me even before his birth. And yes - it was another boy.

Alex was born at home, almost a month late; in the care and delivery of a midwife from beginning to end. It was peaceful to give birth in my own atmosphere with gentle lighting, gentle music and the knowledge of who would be delivering him. He arrived on the living room sofa to the Mozart piano concertos he already loved; his birth witnessed not just by the midwives and Eric; but also by two of his brothers, Stephen and Quinn. They stood with their mouths wide open, hand in hand staring in awe at this miracle. The other children came in immediately after the birth, while the baby was still blue with the umbilical cord still attached. He had been placed on my warm belly, greeted into this world in a great deal of love.

We called Lady Dr. Kim asking her advice on a name. While Eric was on the phone with her, I clearly heard the name Alexander. His Korean name means "new hope, new dawn, new beginning".

I made a birth announcement in calligraphy:

God's hope reborn

New Dawn

In innocent's face

Chapter 22

MUM'S PASSING

Alex was six months old and Kim nearly three when my mother died. I never left any of my children while they were that young and I refused to leave either of these two now. I chose to travel from Boise to Cornwall, a thirty-six hour trip door to door, with them both; Eric staying home with the older children. There were times at the train station, when I simply stood there hoping someone would help me board. This consistently happened, always the right person at the right time.

I arrived in England shortly before my mother died; I knew she waited for me. In great pain with bone cancer, on pretty heavy doses of morphine, she still knew I was coming. She refused the morphine the day we arrived to be sure she was conscious and alert. My Mum had never met Alex and I held him over her bed so she could greet her newest grandson. It was the last time she smiled; even through the pain her delight at seeing him lit up her face.

I received a call the following morning; she had passed away. I had never been around someone who had just died and it was interesting to feel her presence in the room even though she no longer breathed. Her spirit had no idea where to go or what to do so I talked to her to guide her.

I felt her repenting through me, she felt sad that my journey had been difficult. She cried through me for the next few hours. The tears wouldn't stop; all those tears repressed for so long, now pouring from my eyes. She felt sad for having never understood me. She wanted me to stand on the table telling everyone what I had learned and tried to share was real. I explained to her that even though spirit was now obvious to her, my family still thought I was a little crazy and this would just confirm it – big time!

After a while I knew it was time for her to leave and I told her so - but again I felt her confusion, not knowing what to do. I prayed for her; I walked her part way into spirit world and asked for some-one to come for her. I called Eric later and he told me he had been given a vision. He saw her bound with silver cords, being pulled upwards gloriously breaking free of the cords as she went.

I felt much closer to my Mum after she passed. There had always been a barrier between us due to the differences in world views and now that barrier was dissolved.

CONTINUING EDUCATION IN BOISE

Idaho was tough on us, both financially and on our relationship. Eric needed surgery and the insurance company refused to cover it - bills tripled up - collection agencies unrelenting. The pain was both physical and emotional entangling both Eric and me. My back hurt constantly and steadily worsened over the next few years. The Christmas when Alex was one year old, I was unable to pick up a small glass Christmas ornament to place on the tree. I started visiting a chiropractor which helped to a degree but the pain woke me up each night.

Calligraphy became impossible. For Christmas I made a painting for Eric, a combination of calligraphy and water color. "Everything melts into one in true love" was imposed on a background of two koi and water lilies. I was very pleased with it and Eric was moved to tears when I presented it to him. I desperately wanted to create more, but I hurt too much. I was angry, thinking, "Why, just when I am getting good at something I love, do I have to give it up?" It took me a while to find peace with this.

I prolapsed after Alex's birth and Eric and I decided for the sake of my health we would not have any more children. Both of us thought at the beginning of our relationship we would have seven children but that was not to be, this was enough. It was not a hard choice; it felt right on every level, our family was complete.

Our third son was struggling in school so I started teaching him at home. I was introduced to Dorling Kindersley books, birthing a small business selling books and facilitating book parties in people's homes. I had quality books to home-school my children and also made some money. With Eric's surgery over, financially things were settling; he found a job at Micron and kept his part time job presenting the opportunity to buy a house. My business was doing well with all the local libraries buying from me; but I felt spiritually stuck - I no longer felt as if I was moving forwards. Idaho was symbolic to me; the place seemed to be spiritually stagnant, there was a blockage I couldn't get through. Maybe I needed to change perspectives.

I enjoyed selling to libraries and soon found my Dad being a writer was a big help. The first time, I mentioned him coincidentally; however, when I saw the response, I took full advantage. Catherine, the Boise children's librarian, was a sweet woman, small with fine, naturally cut, white hair, not curled as with most people of her generation. I knew her as a librarian and when it came in conversation about my Dad being a writer; I mentioned his best known children's book. Catherine suddenly exclaimed, "I know your father! I took a writers' workshop with him in England years ago - I remember the sparkle in his eyes!" This helped me to step past my shyness and it became easy to sell my books.

Kuna was a unique little place, with an old feed store; a slow, quiet town. It was twenty miles south of Boise and a bubbly, enthusiastic woman ran the library there. She was the sole employee. Anne knew of my Dad's book, 'Jeremy Visick', and was totally delighted in our meeting. "I read it aloud every year to the third grade students! It is my favorite book to read. David Wiseman is wonderful."

Early one afternoon I was driving to Kuna from Boise. It was a beautiful drive, the land was mostly farmland and I opened my window to breathe the freshness in deeply.

I was peaceful driving, reminiscing .... and then God's voice came clearly. I'd been having recurring dreams about a friend from New York, Carrie, for the past week. Carrie was Oliver's wife (the one who had been instrumental in getting Eric and I blessed.) Each night my dream was the same; I saw an open wound on her side that wouldn't heal (she had suffered eight miscarriages).

Spirit asked, "Please have a child for Carrie." I replied, "You're kidding - Now?" I did not doubt where the request was coming from, but I didn't think it was physically possible for me to carry another child. God reiterated, "No, I am not kidding, please have a child for Carrie, it is the only way she can heal. You will have your health back - you will even be able to do your calligraphy." I finally agreed and as I surrendered, I knew how right it was.

I spoke to Eric, and he agreed. Sunday morning, we gathered the kids together and presented the idea to them, when I am pregnant I know everyone sacrifices; half of me is not "there". I was still having personal doubts; you may "know" something but it doesn't mean doubts don't creep in. Stephen, who was all of eleven years old, announced clearly and strongly, "Of *course* you should do it, it is a wonderful thing to do." The tone of his voice and his certainty of spirit reassured my heart. A baby was conceived, unconditionally - the only child I did not have a conscious connection to at the time of conception.

I was not able to give much emotionally to my children during this pregnancy, but one day, Kim, now five years old, came into the bedroom asking, "How come Grandmama is here? And how come she looks so young?"

I knew I had help; Grandmama was the name all of the children called my mother.

The day after Christmas, a little girl was born at home into the arms of her mom and dad, Carrie and Oliver. I looked at them as they held her, the cord still attached to me and it was completely right. She was loved by her mom, her dad, by God and by me in the womb.

OPENING AND MOVING FORWARDS

Post-partum depression crept in. By this time in my life, I had been breast-feeding or pregnant for fifteen years without a break. My body was confused - I had just been pregnant and yet I was not breast-feeding. My husband had not made love to me for the entire pregnancy. The depression strained our relationship even more. He didn't know how to reach me, I was hurt and felt he didn't try; I was far more hurt when he admitted his closeness with another woman. Though he denied any physical connection it explained his separation from me.

I attended a qigong (a Chinese healing exercise) class with a Chinese acupuncturist who had helped me during the pregnancy. Gradually the depression began to lift and nine months later it was gone. My back pain was still very bad but I could see the qigong was helping.

A new chiropractor I went to discovered one of my ribs had been out of position for a very long time. As I reflected back, I thought about my early car crash when I killed the horse. It was after that accident, I ended up in chiropractor's offices. My rib must have been out of place for thirty years, a thirty year lesson to make sure I listened! I was still in chronic pain, but there was hope of healing - God's promise to me was blossoming.

I took fast walks to help get back into shape, using this time to think and pray. It came clear to me that the spiritual blockage I felt before the baby was lifted. There had been something in my lineage that had needed to be cleansed, a payment to be made, and now the bargain was completely satisfied.

It was spring after the birth. Oliver and Carrie had given us a tree for our rather bare yard which we had just planted and I was in the yard watering it. I looked around, visualizing how I would make the simple yard beautiful; where I would put paths among the potential flowers, where I would put a bird bath, how I would plant tall grasses in the corner with a hidden path wandering amongst them and how I would have honeysuckle, with its delightful fragrance I loved so much, climbing up the fence.

I was busy in my imagination when my mother's presence came to me. I felt her delight and her thanks. I didn't realize while I was creating the garden in my mind; but after she thanked me, I knew that my visualizations had actually created this garden for her in spirit world. What I had merely imagined had become real for her.

Not much later Eric and I were offered jobs teaching at a charter school in Arizona. I was grateful to share the financial burden with him. The school was based on the method I used for home-schooling. The children would still have me as their teacher, with a method I trusted, but I would get paid! We sold our house in only two weeks and left for Arizona, the garden never manifesting in this world. It was the first time we moved with a job security at the other end.

ARIZONA

Strangely, the moment we crossed the border to Arizona, Eric and I began communicating with each other again. It was bizarre and we looked at each other in amazement both knowing something had shifted. The charter school did not work out, but it inspired us to move to Prescott where we rapidly made friends. Prescott (nicknamed "Everybody's Home Town") was the first time I have felt "at home".

After the charter school fiasco, we were again in financial straits. For a while I sold roses in the local bars but once Eric found a job at the local mental hospital I worked part time at a health food store selling supplements as well as home-schooling our four younger children.

I continued practicing the qigong I learned in Idaho (Soaring Crane Qigong; a beautiful, elegant form); it helped a little with my back pain but I knew there was something missing. I heard from a co-worker a woman was doing qigong at the town square.

Jenny had only been practicing for six months and was not yet qualified to teach, but she knew the chigong's value and wanted to share it. She practiced in the park, where any-one could join her, and even though she didn't "teach" it, she generously shared. From that first day by the courthouse in the center of Prescott, I never went to the chiropractor again. The pain eased to a point of being bearable.

Jenny told me Luke and Frank Chan, the Chinese brothers who taught her were giving a one day workshop in Phoenix and later in the year they would also be teaching a six day workshop in Sedona. I made the commitment to finding $99.00 for the one day.

As soon as I met Luke in Phoenix I knew I was going to teach Qigong; I would find a way to get the money to go to Sedona. I hadn't doubted the validity of a video showing an ultrasound of a tumor disappearing in under three minutes. When I met Luke, if there had been any inkling of disbelief, it was erased - this man was genuine to the core - and humble! I kept asking myself, "Where is the ego?" Here were just Luke and Frank; kind, loving, sincere and absolutely dedicated to helping people learn to heal themselves.

We had been associated with the Unification Church the whole time we lived in Boise and even when we first arrived in Arizona, but things steadily resonated less.

We tithed for a long time, but then it no longer felt right. I realized it had become a crutch; I knew if I gave my ten percent faithfully, money would come back, but now I saw it was being given out of fear. Besides, ten percent was no longer enough according to Rev. Moon, and members were being asked to give thirty percent.

It was pretty impossible to do enough in the Unification Church; it was set up that way. Rev. Moon, at first, said you should sleep only four hours a night, I never managed this, (though I was always a little guilty about the fact) but some people did. Then Rev. Moon informed us he was now only sleeping one hour. As people reached an exceedingly high standard, it was again no longer good enough. One blessing ceremony was no longer enough; there were now three to guarantee you did everything you were supposed to; it kept getting more and more difficult. The door which Rev. Moon had opened was now blocked. He was not letting people through, but was standing, massively; his ego blocking the way.

Chapter 26

There came a time of distinct separation between myself and the Unification Church. Members were being directed to go to South America where Rev. Moon had acquired land in Paraguay. The message came for everyone to go and help for a while. When you arrived in Paraguay, you were to sign a book and you would be guaranteed a place in the Kingdom of Heaven. This repelled me; not only did it not resonate, it felt entirely wrong, it disgusted me.

The parallel to indulgences, (before the reformation of the church by Martin Luther, when people would buy their way into the Kingdom of Heaven,) wouldn't leave my mind. I was sickened and it was then I determined not to walk any part of my life out of fear, but only out of love. I would live my own truth, and I would walk my walk because of my absolute *love* of God, nothing else. If I didn't go to the Kingdom of Heaven, so be it. As a great blues player once said, "If the truth is going to send me to hell, them I'm hell bound." It was hard separating from the Unification Church, there was so much guilt. Fear of failure and judgment were embedded in the teachings which had insidiously become ingrained in my thinking. It took a great deal of strength to step away.

A couple of years later, I returned to Idaho to hear Rev. Moon speak. I was no longer active in the church, but much of what I had learned, both good and bad, stayed with me. I arrived at the hotel the evening before he was scheduled to speak and waited in line beside a Korean state leader who encouraged me to go to pledge early the next morning. He told me that everyone was invited. It seemed like a good idea, so I got up the next morning at 3:30 a.m. and did my wall squats. Feeling balanced and ready, I went to the suite where the ceremony was to be held. I wondered if I had the right room - there were the typical "guards", but no lines of people and very few of the inevitable shoes left outside the door. The guard, a young church brother, saw my hesitancy, but said, "Do you want to go in?" I did.

Rev. and Mrs. Moon were not there yet; just a few church elders. I kept expecting more people to turn up, but they didn't. It was just me, along with church leaders (most of whom were Korean and all of whom were men.) I felt awkward and when Rev. Moon and his wife entered, I realized no-one else was coming. There was no way out; I fudged my way through pledge (spoken in Korean) - actually I simply mumbled unintelligible sounds hoping no-one would notice. It took me quite a while to stop questioning why I was there and to realize I was exactly where I was supposed to be. After pledge, Rev. Moon gave a talk (all in Korean) and while I couldn't understand a word, I made a very deep prayer, connecting with him.

Later, in the large conference room, during his public talk, (which was in English and where there were far more people), Rev. Moon turned and looked penetratingly at me through the crowd, "You don't need the Messiah," he said, "You just need to love your children." It was good to have the affirmation of what I already knew intuitively and the residual guilt faded away.

He also said how he was an old man and people did not have to listen to him. Unfortunately, members of the Unification Church couldn't let him go and kept feeding into something which should have evolved long before.

CHI-LEL QIGONG

I practiced Chi-Lel qigong consistently each day committing to one hundred consecutive days. My pain became manageable; I was healthier in every way.

I heard Philip B. was doing work channeling Saint Germain in Phoenix. Eric and I were intrigued and went to a few meetings. He had been one of the respected elders of the Unification Church, now being separated from it.

The first meditation with him led us through woods, along a path and up wide steps leading to a mansion; we entered a room filled with great spiritual leaders. We were asked to choose whomever we wished to talk to. I elected to speak with Paramahansa Yogananda, but as I started to converse with him he told me I should be talking to Jesus.

Jesus told me I should just be kind and loving. I expressed to him I didn't like the guilt I carried inside me, the self- judgment I still lived with on a daily basis. Jesus replied, "That doesn't come from me, or from your Father." I had to reflect on where it was coming from, certainly not from anywhere positive. The inner conflict was somewhat eased and knew I no longer had to listen to my self doubts. I realized not only did I need to be kind and loving to others but also to myself. I had to learn to stop judging myself, to get off my own back.

The second time we visited Philip was towards the end of my one hundred day practice of qigong. On day ninety-five I had really bad diarrhea. A couple of nights later, I couldn't sleep, as the cleansing had continued; I was pretty depleted with intense stomach cramps. I quit trying to sleep, got out of bed at 3:00am and did some wall squats. As I lay back down I had a vision of Dr. Pang Ming, Lao

Shi, (who was the one who developed the Chi-Lel in China).

He showed me the beauty of a cricket, also the beauty of a rose with a dew drop on it. He took me to the ocean and I swam and we rode on the back of dolphins (interesting since water and swimming were still areas that caused some fear for me - but I was not afraid). He took me to a precipitous cliff I was to climb (heights were another one of my untamed fears). Every rock was exquisitely beautiful, - bejeweled and glistening, I climbed up, even scaling some parts upside down and yet no fear. When we reached the top, I tried riding a tiger, but Dr. Pang said, "Why the tiger?" I realized it was not true to this experience, but instead something I thought I "should" experience because of one of Rev. Moon's talks on Spirit World. It was my brain getting in the way, trying to control the experience rather than simply allowing it.

I again found myself at the bottom of the cliff and re-climbed its beautiful face effortlessly. This time as I reached the top, Dr. Pang said, "We must hurry". I had stopped and declared, "But, it is so beautiful here". He reiterated insistently, "No, we must hurry!" So we ran, incredibly fast, streaming with blurred multi-colors on either side of us. Suddenly we broke through into a place of absolute calm, absolute stillness, where there were multitudes of stars; I looked at him and I asked, "Who *are* you?"

"I am God's son," he replied, "And you are God's daughter." "Now," he continued, "The trick is to bring all of this back inside".

As I came back into my body, all the pain was gone. Dr. Pang taught me the essence of Chi-Lel; to think out to the universe, connecting with universal energy and then to think inside the body, allowing it to penetrate deeply, bringing the harmony of the universe into my being.

The following day I had a fever and thought there was no way we could go to see Philip as planned, I lay down to rest but felt an urgency to practice Chi-Lel instead. By the end of the form, my fever was gone and I felt completely normal. In the evening of my ninety-ninth day we drove to Phoenix.

Philip was preparing to channel St. Germain and he greeted the people coming in from the spirit world, Jesus, Mother Theresa, Sir Arthur Conan Doyle, Young Oon Kim and Tiger Pak (Unification Church elders). He said they were all sitting on a grassy slope. I experienced this and was drawn to Jesus. I sat by his feet as he took my left hand and Mother Theresa took my right. Jesus told me to use his hands when I healed, as my desire is to heal not only physically but spiritually. On my one hundredth day of practice, Jesus came to me; he super-imposed himself on me, practicing the form with me.

The money for the six day workshop with Luke and Frank Chan manifested; nothing would have stopped me and with that intention, the money turned up. The workshop site was magnificent, outside of Sedona among the red rocks. I was still extremely shy and felt awkward being with a group of people I didn't know, but a wonderful Hawaiian man greeted me with great warmth, teaching me to hug heart to heart.

The bond with Luke Chan was deep; I prayed, contemplating this bond. I asked God what was this I felt with Luke and I was told, "He is like your brother, yet more than your brother, your twin." I also asked Spirit how the Chi Lel could be so powerful in America. I was told it was because of the two brothers, Luke and Frank together; how the unity between them allowed Spirit to work.

Being a dedicated student; I was always first back to class after a break. Luke would sit, patiently while people gathered. He gently practiced a neck movement while waiting and, as I was always there too, I did the same movement. By the end of the six days of this practice with Luke I had a blue image in my head of the pattern of that movement, a blue infinity sign, imposed in my brain. I later realized Luke is my intuitive teacher; I learn intuitively from him and he can impart knowledge to me this way.

He had an innate joy and lightness about him; he was my best friend even though I barely knew him. One lunch time, Luke had been given a bowl of little silver fish and discovering I liked them, he came over, delightfully scooping half of them onto my plate, giggling as he did so.

I called Luke, "Mr. Chi" as I felt waves of chi emanating from him. One time as we sat in a circle, he knew I was in great pain, and as he sent chi around the group, I felt him focus on me; he looked at me and asked "do you feel better now?" I certainly did!

Luke had made a forty-five minute tape of affirmations he was really proud of. We used it over and over throughout the workshop. It was called "The Journey to Health and Happiness". On the last day, Luke wanted us to do a practice for the whole length of the tape; it could be anything we had learned, our choice. I knew I couldn't do wall squats for that long, and with my back injury I certainly couldn't sustain any of the arm movements for more than a couple of minutes; so my only option was push up and down. This is where you bend over with your hands on your feet and press up and down. I did this, for forty-five minutes! Legs far too straight, form totally wrong, but I kept going for the whole tape. I was so pleased when the tape ended, I had done it. Until I tried to stand back up! I was stuck and couldn't move. The only way was to fall to the side. So, slightly embarrassed, I tipped over, catching myself rather inelegantly, much to the great amusement of

Luke. I also felt he was proud of me; I had gone beyond a barrier in myself and I felt high; I felt a great sense of achievement and renewal.

When Eric picked me up he could not deny the change in me. As we drove back along the seemingly endless dirt road we were waved to a stop by a Hopi man. He showed us a snake that had been hit; he stopped us to allow him time to get it out of the way. He gently lifted the snake off the road with great respect and took it to a safer place to be honored. Both Eric and I knew this was significant; the snake being a sign of rebirth.

I kept practicing Chi Lel every day, doing many one hundred day gongs of different movements. One of the first phenomenal shifts was that I began to trust the universe. As I let go to universal energy, I felt supported and no longer alone. I learned to relax, releasing even more. One of the most powerful gongs was a practice to the "Journey to Health and Happiness" tape, I did a simple hip rotation for the full forty-five minutes for a hundred consecutive days. Old sexual trauma was released along with many other emotions I didn't even realize were trapped in my body. I sobbed my way through the first eighty days feeling wonderful when I finished!

My back became rapidly stronger. I had previously come to the conclusion during my journey with chiropractors that healing took a long time. Chi-Lel made me re-think that statement, healing was happening quickly! My practice also became an internal haven for me, a place of peace I would retreat to each day.

I attended another six day workshop; this one at Mount Shasta as I felt a pressing need to be certified at the earliest possible opportunity. I had practiced for a year.

Luke, seeing my dedication, certified me to teach level one of Chi-Lel qigong in August 1999.

I missed everyone and would talk to Eric and the kids each evening. It was especially hard being separated from Alex as he was the youngest. We learned to do chi hugs over the telephone; I pictured myself hugging Alex while I mustered all the chi I could gather to give him. He felt these hugs very strongly as did his sister and when I returned home we continued the tradition of chi hugs from across the room. It was something tangible to all of us and a good lesson in non-locality – you don't have to be physically close to be connected.

I spent a lot of time alone at the workshop, finding a spot on a rock by a stream and spending most moments not involving qigong practice praying and just being. As before, this workshop gave me exactly what I needed; an internal, quiet peace. At each workshop I learned to see more of my value, who *I* was, not just who I was in my marriage. I started to see myself more clearly. I also came to know Frank Chan and I much appreciated his quiet wisdom. He was the one people went to when they were struggling and he was always there with what was needed, always loving, always encouraging.

I loved my qigong practice, I felt harmonized and there was the beginning of a sense of something more inside me. I knew this was God's promise; but it was not just my back that was receiving healing.

I learned through a chiropractor in Boise how everything is interconnected, how our emotions often manifest in sickness, so to receive healing we need to work on the whole picture. To clean out physical sickness we have to work through our emotional body.

ChiLel chigong facilitates healing on every level, physical, emotional and mental.

The Story of Alexander

CRISIS

A month later, in September, 1999, we took a trip to Big Sur, California. Alex was ill, his appetite was terrible; pale as he was I still thought he was okay. We played on the beach, he drew crabs in the sand with a stick but his stamina just wasn't what it should be. On the drive home, I intuitively felt the presence of a Tibetan Lama with me; I thought it was the one who refused me his blessing so many years ago in Darjeeling. He was sorry he had not been there for me then and he reassured me he was there now. I felt his presence with me for a long time, but didn't understand why he had come after so very many years.

It was during that vacation I knew something was seriously wrong with Alex, but denial is strong and I still convinced myself it was nutritional. Eric and I had made plans to go to Hawaii for a "honeymoon" in the fall as we had never had one. We took the trip to Big Sur in September as a family, so the children would be O.K. with us doing this for ourselves. Great friends, Robin and Charlie planned to stay with the children, so everything was covered.

But something was terribly wrong. Alex had been throwing up, it looked as if he had a stomach virus but I intuitively knew it was more. The word leukemia came to mind. Alex pleaded, "Do you have to go? When I feel so sick?" I didn't want to leave him and it tore at my heart. Eric was insistent and became angry. "You don't care about us," he yelled, "You only care about the children."

So, I went to Hawaii, even though I was tremendously conflicted.

Maui was beautiful; we stayed on the jungle side, the gentle warm Hawaiian breeze whispering its melody through the palm fronds. There were many "coincidences", connections with some-one from Truro where I grew up, people giving me jewelry, welcoming me, sharing Aloha. The signs were so numerous I thought we should move there.

Hawaii welcomed me but it also enhanced the disharmony in our relationship. Eric and I were in constant conflict, a honeymoon with no romance.

Near our lodgings was a kiva, a circular room used for meditation. We were invited to join an early morning meditation on our third day of vacation. As I sat, the energy opened my heart chakra. I felt it open, completely. I knew this was the reason I was there.

I called home regularly, each time being assured everything was O.K. Robin had taken Alex to a naturopath. She thought he was anemic, advising us to get a blood test taken on our return to Prescott. When I called the third day, after the meditation, Robin stated, "It is time for you to come home." I heard an urgency in her voice which resonated with the one in my own heart.

We drove to the airport as quickly as possible boarding the first available plane on an emergency ticket. Eric decided to stay in Hawaii saying he could pray more clearly for Alex there. Robin and Alex met me at the airport. He looked incredibly fragile and I held him, praying. When we reached home, Alex ate a little yogurt; I would take him in the morning for the blood test.

It was dark, completely quiet. Robin and Charlie had gone home, the children were asleep, Alex on my bed.

I sat at the computer in need of support, on the verge of panic and wrote an email to Luke Chan and posted a message to the forum asking for chi energy.

"Dear Luke,
I wanted to ask if you could please send chi to our six year old son, Alex. He is very weak and is eating and drinking very little. He is extremely pale and is getting very bad headaches. We took him to a naturopathic doctor and she said he is severely anemic. We have to do blood work on Monday. Anemia can be a sign of another disease - some are not so serious, some are very serious.
Anyway - please send him some chi.
Thank you Luke,
Much chi,
Deborah "

This was the first of many messages and the beginning of an incredible depth of support for this little boy. I returned to the bedroom snuggling with Alex; he had a bad headache and wasn't sleeping well. There was some blood around his mouth, I was getting scared. He had been having severe nose bleeds recently. Suddenly he vomited a copious amount of blood. It was old blood, swallowed from a nose bleed going down the back of his throat.

I called Charlie and soon he was carrying Alex to the emergency room. The E.R. doctors took a blood sample from his thigh causing a huge, swelling hematoma. His blood counts were so low he had no platelets to enable it to clot. I finally gave voice to my fear, "Could it be leukemia?" "It might be," came the reply.

They wanted to give him a blood transfusion in Prescott, informing me he would need several, but fortunately they called the oncology doctor on call in Phoenix first. She said wait, just get him to Phoenix

Children's Hospital as quickly as possible. We were air-lifted to Phoenix by helicopter. It was debatable if I would be able to go with him, but I begged the helicopter pilot. He looked at me and asked how heavy I was, "115 pounds" I lied. I was told "O.K. you can come".

Charlie returned to the house to grab my still-packed suitcase, driving to join us in Phoenix. Robin stayed with the other children. Spirit was with me, allowing me to be with Alex, to arrive back from Hawaii before he went into crisis and putting in place the support we needed.

It was close to dawn when we arrived at the hospital. Alex was rushed to intensive care, pads stuck all over him to monitor his vital signs. Charlie arrived and I managed to get a phone call to Eric, also to my sister in England. I tried to call my Dad, willing him to pick up the phone, but in England it was already late and he was in bed.

One of my fears had been that I may not be able to stay with Alex but the reality was completely different. The ICU nurse encouraged me to lie on the bed with him and hold him. Charlie was wonderful, he seemed normal and "up", Charlie just being Charlie. His natural curiosity about what was happening both charmed the nurse and kept me from retreating into the black hole of fear.

Late morning, I met Dr. Singer and her team; Renee, the social worker and Annie, the nurse. They were supportive and calm; I trusted them. I began to feel safe, my guard down, until Dr. Singer told me it was touch and go as to whether he would make it or not. She meant to be encouraging when she said, "Even children who are this sick can sometimes pull through".

It hit me like a ton of bricks - I knew he was very sick, but the possibility he might die had not entered my mind; I felt extreme guilt that I had been in Hawaii, not acknowledging the severity of his illness. Why hadn't I taken him to a doctor earlier? Suddenly the symptoms seemed so obvious - how could I have failed to see how sick he was? He had bruises, but we had recently moved to our new house where he played outside a lot more. He had nose-bleeds, but we live at six thousand feet elevation and he had allergies (both of which can be the cause). Where had he crossed the line from being fair-skinned to white, from having a bad appetite to hardly eating? The changes had been slow and subtle. I had intuitively known but hadn't wanted to see, and the power of denial blinded me.

Here we were, in ICU with nurses trying to push thick, yellow blood products into his veins while he screamed in pain and fear. What could I say when he asked, "Why me? Why am I going through this?" I wished I knew. I prayed and told God, "I know I will grow from this, I will be a better person because of this, but that is NOT enough. There *has* to be more reason for his suffering. It has to be bigger than my growth and my family's growth." All I could do was pray and surround him with as much peace as possible.

Another doctor came in and shared something which helped alleviate the guilt that was blocking me from giving everything I could to Alex. I *needed* to hear what he had to tell me. "Almost all children with leukemia go into crisis before they are diagnosed. Even if I had brought Alex in a week before, a blood test may not have been conclusive. He would still have to go through this, the treatment would have been the same." Some of my guilt abated and I was able to come out of my self-absorption and focus on my son.

Alex tried to sit up but swooned and collapsed. For a second, I thought he died but slowly his eyes re-opened. I was more than just grateful to Charlie. He was my life-line. While in his company I was okay, but when I was alone it became unbearable - even in the short time it took me to go to the bathroom.

How could I help my son? How could I take his pain? I tried to fill him with Chi, concentrating on the Chi field, bringing in the peaceful energy I knew, creating a safe place for him. I couldn't do the form in the ICU, but I could do it in my mind, so I visualized Alex and me practicing together. I tried to will the sickness away. I thought that if my love totally surrounded Alex, he wouldn't hurt as much. When he felt my presence intensely, he did feel better; it was obvious he was more relaxed and felt safer. Every part of my energy and strength focused.

Robin posted another message on the forum for me:
"I am writing on the behalf of Alex Lucas who is a beautiful six year old boy whose family has just learned that he has leukemia. Alex is at Phoenix Children's hospital in Arizona, where he was taken once the severity of his illness was discovered early this morning. Please help him and his family by sending LOTS OF LOVING CHI!

Alex, his family and I send you many thanks for your willingness to be so caring and giving. May you be blessed for your help!"

Eric returned from Hawaii as soon as he could; I thought everything would be easier with him there, with his support, but I was wrong. I was not able to encompass him. His trip had been tortuous, filled with prayer and turmoil. I needed him to stand with me in strength. As I held the place of calm for Alex, Eric felt cut out, his anger and frustration at the situation making me protect Alex even more.

Messages of support had been coming back since the first message I posted, Robin faxed them to the hospital. I was not alone, the power of the chi field supported me.

When Alex stabilized we were transferred to the pediatric cancer ward for the next six days. There was a cot provided for me to sleep. Our room-mate was a little baby, about four months old who had a tumor behind one eye. The parents and grandparents reached out beyond their own situation and encompassed our family; they greeted us, showing their concern. This family moved my heart deeply; I was not able to go beyond my own situation yet this family could, they went beyond their pain. Believe me; I needed the big hug I received from the baby's grandmother. They helped me to see a bigger picture, one large enough to encompass Eric a little, one where I could see there was still a world beyond the reality of Alex and myself.

I practiced Chi-lel in my mind as often as possible and telephoned Luke Chan to ask for his help. Luke told me emphatically to visualize Alex as healthy. But it was too hard. I expressed this to Luke and he advised me to visualize him, not lying in bed healthy, but jumping on the trampoline. I tried, I know how important positive visualization is, but I couldn't shake the images out of my head; I started verbally, saying over and over, "Alex is healed, Alex is healthy". This way the energy coming in would reinforce a positive view and I could keep the sick images out.

I learned to trick my brain and visualized him growing up which helped as it was distant from the present reality. I saw him as a healthy teenager, as a healthy young man (with a beard) and as a father of his own children

I now understood the power of chi energy more. Alex needed a port-a-cath inserted under his skin allowing direct access to his veins. We knew this procedure was necessary, his veins so tired they couldn't take any more medication pushed through them. He was still extremely weak to go through surgery.

We were allowed in the pre-surgery room, not just myself and Eric, but also his brothers Stephen and Quinn and his sister Kim. He was surrounded by love. I prayed desperately and reached to the chi field in China, pulling chi into the room with every ounce of intense concentration. My focus was absolute as I envisioned the thousands of people practicing in the hospital in China, bringing the energy generated by so many into the hospital in Phoenix.

When I opened my eyes, Alex had pink cheeks and red lips - he had been white until then (even his lips had been drained of color). We were all amazed; Eric and the children had watched as the color gradually appeared. I *knew* he would come out of the surgery okay. but I continued focusing on bringing chi throughout the procedure.

I wrote another message to the forum. Individuals, families, and groups all sent chi, from different parts of America, Canton and Malaysia. Malaysia brought the support of a group of two hundred people.

Over the next few days I continued visualizing Alex and myself together practicing the form. I also played the "Chi Field Chant"; a C.D. an American woman, (who had experienced her own healing in China with Dr. Pang) made. It repeated the Chinese words for bringing in the chi field. Whenever I played it, Alex slept better. I put the tape on whenever I woke in the night - I knew it kept the chi energy in the room - even when I was too exhausted to bring it in myself. Fortunately the people sharing the room also loved the chant. Initially, I played it very quietly so as not to disturb them, but then they asked me to increase the volume.

The world of childhood cancer is not one anyone wishes to enter. I had seen children in the store, bald due to chemotherapy and although I always felt bad for them, I was distant, grateful it wasn't my own child. Well, now it *was* my child and somehow this world was not as bad as I had imagined - it was filled with wonderful people, exceptional people, doctors and nurses who never held back their hearts.

The nurses are trained to give the children as many choices as possible. Alex needed medication, but if he wasn't ready for some procedure, they always gave him time to adjust; they gave him as much power over his situation as they could.

A friend, Jane, came to the hospital. At this time of extreme circumstance, I found the right people already in place. I don't know how we would have coped had Robin and Charlie had not been in our lives and with Jane it was similar; she was always there. I never doubted I could call her day or night. She seemed to know exactly what I was going through at any given moment intuitively knowing the right thing to say or do. She helped me see Eric's frustration as normal and she told me (though I didn't listen to this one immediately) I needed to get out of the hospital room for a while.

The whole thing was a very humbling experience. We tend to think we live such independent lives, but it is an illusion; we need each other, every person who comes into our life. That interconnection became crystal clear. The person who cleaned the room was fundamental to my life, not just because the room was clean, but because of who they were, the smile they gave. A look of compassion or a kind word meant so much I was often moved to the verge of tears.

On one occasion, because of anxiety, Alex was given the drug adavan to calm him; it was supposed to calm him but instead of getting sleepy, Alex got "high". This child in a wheel chair, who hadn't walked for several days, or had the strength to sit up, suddenly decided to race around and around the nurse's station (still in the wheel chair). He was laughing and giggling, "Whee! I'm flying! I'm in happy land," he repeated over and over. "I'm in happy land!" Eric and I were rolling with laughter, along with the nurses and his brothers and sister. It was a relief to laugh.

As Alex became stronger, the nurses encouraged us to visit the children's ward; the children's cancer ward was one floor above the regular children's ward. We took what seemed like a major excursion down to the play room. Alex's energy was drained by the time we arrived, but the room was cheerful, kind volunteers helped the children with activities.

We sat at a small table and Eric found paper and markers. Alex wanted us to make a paper airplane which Eric did. That part met with his approval, but then came the coloring. He was so sick, absolutely on edge, the effects of prednisone beginning to kick in. I later learned his platelets were low, and when that happened he was even edgier, it gave him a "creeping" feeling.

He wanted me to make an 'H' on the wing of the plane and as I tried to draw one for him, he screamed at me -"NOT like that." This sweet child, who had up until now been so patient, was in an absolute rage, the first of many induced by the prednisone. It shook us all, including Alex. He took a piece of paper and drew a shaky bubble "H". I understood what he wanted and drew one as perfectly as possible on the wing of the airplane. He relaxed a little, but then he wanted me to color the whole plane black, leaving the 'H' white. I thought it would be fairly easy, but I soon found he wanted the plane to be *completely* black - not one white spot allowed to show through. The markers didn't work very well but I kept coloring; totally intent on making it perfect. He was too weak to color it himself, but he wanted it exactly as he pictured it in his mind. Every time there was a tiny spot of white, he got extremely upset.

Alex had always been a very gentle-natured, calm boy and to see him like this was hard to comprehend. But, we kept going. Each time his anger rose, his nose started to bleed, and while I colored, Eric grabbed tissues to staunch the flow. We sat for about a half hour, dedicated to coloring, while blood poured during his regular outbursts of tears and frustration. I became more focused and more and more careful. Finally, he relaxed visibly, the last specks of white filled in.

Our energy totally expended we headed back to the room; paper airplane in tow. He turned to me, pleased the airplane turned out so well and said, "I want Kim to have this, because she is the most worried." Sick as he was, he still thought about his sister. It was good to know beneath the rage he was still Alex. His attitude throughout his ordeal never ceased to amaze me. Many times it was he who kept me going, not the other way around.

Three days before his seventh birthday, on October 17th, he was released from hospital and we went home, at least for a while. We had only been in the hospital for a week, but it seemed like an eternity. We were greeted by a house full of welcome home signs which Robin, Charlie and the kids had made.

Alex returned to Phoenix for a lumbar puncture which showed he was going into remission and was responding to the chemotherapy. The future was to consist of intensive chemotherapy for the next twenty-eight days, three times a week and then regular chemotherapy for the next nine months and occasionally over the next three years. I felt "we can do this," it may not be the future we had anticipated, but it was a future. I knew it would be hard but did not seem unbearable. The cure rate was eighty percent and I was certain of his recovery.

The day we arrived home, a family of javelina visited us, several of them wandering through the yard. Our house backs onto the forest and they are not infrequent visitors; they come through looking for food or sometimes simply lie around and rest for a while. This time, they had two babies with them, tiny brown babies, lovingly protected by the whole pack. The mother brought them right up to the french doors. Usually the babies are kept more distant, not pushed to the forefront, but there they were as if they were being introduced to Alex, noses against the glass. The mother was saying, "There he is!"

SOMEWHAT HARDER

Oliver, (the father of the baby born in Boise) called; he always seems to call when important. I told him I was confident we could handle this, I was sure Alex would recover without complications. He said he was sorry, but he felt there was more, it was not going to be that simple.

With the warning in the back of my mind (about as far back as I could shove it), ten days after his diagnosis we still had a celebratory birthday, filled with joy and laughter. We were very grateful he was *having* a birthday. Things moved on, we gave him a short buzz haircut in preparation for his inevitable hair loss. He was extremely "cool" about it. When his hair started to fall out he danced around pretending to be a monkey, pulling it out by the handful!

On October 26th, Alex got a fever; we had been warned of this. The chemo demolished his white blood cell counts enabling infection to set in. When his fever rose to over one hundred degrees we headed back to Phoenix (a two hour trip), packed and ready for the hospital.

There was road construction along much of I-17 in Phoenix, the traffic abruptly stopped; Eric avoided the car in front of us but we were rear-ended by a guy on a cell phone. Alex's temperature was now almost 103 degrees. Finally, we made it to the hospital in time for Alex to get antibiotics intravenously breaking his fever. I was back in a hospital room; same uncomfortable cot, same lack of sleep, nurses coming in at odd times of the night. I began to resign myself to the situation. I learned to say, "Whatever", and I began the difficult, but ultimately rewarding, process of learning I am not in control. We stayed in the hospital until October 30th.

Halloween was magical. Robin and Charlie had taken Stephen, Quinn and Kim shopping while we were in the hospital. They brought back an assorted array of hideous things - spiders (along with lots of webbing), bats, eyeballs etc. and together designed a haunted house. Obviously with Alex, we couldn't go trick or treating, but not one of them complained - they just changed their way of thinking, making one hallway of the house into a haunted area. Each sibling dressed up as something scary; Kim a ghost, Quinn a vampire and Stephen a mummy. Their plan was for Alex to be given some special object enabling him to defeat each monster. He was given a pillow to defeat the ghost in one bedroom, a cross to defeat the vampire in the other bedroom and a plastic toy "idol" to defeat the mummy who lurked in the bathroom. As he disappeared through the draped, spidery web, I heard screams of delight and feigned horror - they were having a wonderful time. When Alex emerged, victorious from his battles, his face beamed. "They did all that for me!" he pronounced.

There was another week of chemo to get through, but Alex's heart was lighter. He was always with both Eric and me as well as with his siblings; if he was at the clinic, so were we, when he was hospitalized, we were all with him. We were family.

The level of support increased and deepened. Messages continued to come in from the forum. Luke led healing circles for Alex every night and the energy being sent to us was obvious. I considered taking him to see Luke, but his immune system was so weakened by the chemotherapy I decided it was best not to. One thing that helped keep me going was a visualization of the next year's workshop in Sedona. I pictured myself, standing with a healthy Alex, thanking everyone for making it possible.

Other people also became involved; people in our community were tremendous with prayer, food and offers of fund-raising help coming in.

Herman Shorty, a Navajo medicine man heard of Alex through a friend of ours. Herman had never met Alex and it was almost two years before I met him. But even without a personal connection to any of us, he took Alex into his heart, organizing a sweat lodge on the Navajo reservation. He gathered together twenty-one men and led a ceremony for our son's healing. I told this to a friend some time later and he said, "You mean he cared that much?" This Navajo medicine man cared deeply for a little seven year old white boy he had not even met.

Later, Herman came to lead a sweat lodge ceremony in Prescott; to connect it spiritually to the one on the reservation. He used the same sweet grass he used on the reservation which he then gave to Eric. We put this on an altar kept in the hospital room, along with other gifts of healing which were given to us. Herman gave us his piercing sticks from his second Sundance to give us strength; one for Eric and one for myself.

On November 9th Alex had another lumbar puncture to check for remission. This was standard procedure a month after diagnosis. I was concerned, but not worried. The doctor's expression was not good, then came those dreaded words, "I am so sorry." The world stopped, and it became hard to breathe. Outside the room, the first people we met were the parents of the little baby who had been our first roommate. They looked me in the eye and said with great strength, "Never give up". I knew they were right.

I wrote another message to the forum:
"My Dear Chi-Lel Friends,

I debated about putting this posting because I know people turn to the forum for inspiration, and I felt that I wasn't going to be able to share that, but I know how much I love Chi-Lel and how much I believe in chi. I have been pain free for a year after having chronic back pain for 23 years, and I have grown a full inch in height. But my situation right now does not involve my own healing.

Alex (aged 7) did not respond to the month of chemotherapy for his leukemia. I felt for sure he was in remission because he felt so much better, but his energy obviously came from chi and prayers rather than his leukemia getting better. Tomorrow, we have to take him to Phoenix Children's Hospital for 5 days of really intense chemo. The doctors (who are truly filled with great love and compassion) are going to try to knock the leukemia cells out. After 28 days of therapy, 66% of his cells are still leukemia blast cells. At this point 99% of children with leukemia are usually in remission; unfortunately this percentage does not include Alex. If they succeed in getting him into remission with this treatment, they will do a bone marrow transplant. They can't do a transplant until he goes into remission.

Does the fact that he has leukemia mean that all the chi sent to him didn't work - ABSOLUTELY NOT - it made a huge difference. We could feel the chi in the hospital with him (being sent from all over the world) and we could feel the chi in the house all around him, especially being sent from the Sedona workshop. Thank you again Luke and Frank and everyone involved. Alex has energy where he should have none, and most of all he is happy and has very few direct side effects.

I want to ask that anyone who feels called to do so please join us in this fight. There is still a chance for him and I absolutely believe in chi and in miracles. The chemo will take five days, but then his body will be totally wiped out, and he will remain hospitalized for 2-3 weeks, so that his body can recover strength. If he does not go into remission, then there is nothing else medical science can do. PLEASE, help us in this battle, chi truly is an incredible weapon and each and every person who is in the chi field is amazing.

May loving chi live in and be expressed though us all, With much love, Deborah."

In less than two hours messages of support started coming in.

Becci: *"I meet with a group tomorrow evening and we will definitely send some group chi your way - your message has been an inspiration...... You are showing us not to give up but to look for the best and to expect the best....."*

Irene: *"We are sending you loving chi every day from New York City. Imagine that Alex is well, that all the blood cells are normal, that all leukemia cells are normal, have disappeared, and that you are completely healthy. Think of yourself (and your son) as being healthy and able to fight it. Many millions of people love you."*

Joel: *"Tonight and tomorrow night during our practice, my group from Penang, Malaysia will send Alex healing chi. We want Alex to know that he is NOT ALONE, we are with him."*

Even with this support, I barely made it back to the hospital; Eric was parking the car, it was just Alex and me. I slowly pushed the wheel chair onto the elevator. I could hardly breathe as I entered, knowing the doctors were going to use heavy chemo to shock the cancer into remission. His chances of living getting smaller. I reached into my purse and held the piercing stick Herman had given me. It was truly amazing how the strength suffused my being and I was able to breathe deeply; my tears receded. By the time the elevator stopped at the cancer ward, I was strong. Many, many times I held that precious piercing stick; some days I barely put it down. If I felt weak, it gave me strength. I felt Herman's prayer and love for Alex.

MIRACLES

M ore messages kept coming, Robin faxed them to me in the hospital, and I read each one to Alex.

Luke Chan wrote: *"Dear Deborah, You are a beautiful soul and an inspiration to all of us. We are standing by you and your family to bring Alex back to your loving arms. Pang Lao-Shi, all of us, 10 million practitioners are surrounding Alex now and are continuously sending him loving healing chi until he returns to being a normal healthy boy.*
Hao La! Hao La! Hao La!
Luke"

Hao La is a Chinese word meaning it is already accomplished.

Yapp Laixing wrote: *"We in Malaysia are all with you and Alex, the world and the whole universe are as well. We are sure you can do it and your son can make it too, no doubt about it. Harmony/healing chi is with you Alex."*

Nancy wrote: *"Dear Deborah, You are not alone. I felt the chi at the Sedona workshop, you and Alex were right there with us. I do Chi-Lel with three different groups and you and Alex are included each time in my daily practice. My prayers are with you. You are in my heart.*
Much love and compassion and much healing chi,
Nancy, CA."

People sent healing stories of others to inspire me. I grew to love these wonderful people on the forum. They became family.

The only time I started to give up hope, (it was just starting to creep in, not really formed in my mind, but was knocking at the door), Luke called. The moment doubt tried to make its way into my conscious thoughts, there was Luke not allowing it. I was not able to go to a negative place, I was held strong by Spirit, through the numerous people in the chi field. Luke emphasized I could NOT go into negative thinking and advised me to put requests for specific chi on the forum. Everyone would be visualizing with the same intention which would magnify the results. I did this, requesting each person visualize ALL the leukemia cells being killed by the chemotherapy.

The chemo was extremely strong, but intuitively I knew it was necessary. I emitted chi energy into each bag of chemo as it came into the hospital room; I connected to the chi field and allowed the beautiful, pure energy to gather and focus in the medicine, transforming it into something positive. This stuff *looked* evil, but I tried my best to get past that. I sent a prayer for the chemo to do exactly what it needed with as little damage to the rest of his body as possible. It was powerful to focus in this way.

The chemo treatment was set to finish on the 17th but on the 16th we received more devastating information; not only had the cancer not gone into remission, the doctors had also found a rare abnormality in the leukemia cells called a 4/11 translocation. These children virtually always die. I needed to put another message on the forum.

"Dear Friends, I am so moved by your responses - Thank you once again. The last couple of messages were relayed from me through a friend as I am basically cut off while at the hospital, but I have found internet access through the library here.

Alex is almost through the intensive chemo, as of about 3:00 in the morning Arizona time he will be finished.

They don't know if he will go into remission from that, not yet, but the feeling of my husband and I is by doing this, we have bought time for chi to work. The chances of Alex's survival - even if we did the bone marrow are less than 0.02%, and should he survive, the chances of his having all kinds of problems from the bone marrow are huge. He has a 4/11 translocation in the chromosomes of the leukemia cells that make his type of leukemia virtually impossible to treat. But, chi does work, '101 Miracles' is a book full of just that - miracles. I asked Luke about the possibility of taking him to China, but that is out right now, in his condition the trip alone could be very dangerous. So - if we can't go to China, then China will have to come to us - and I know it can, with your help.

When this round of chemo is over we need to visualize only normal healthy cells will return, NO leukemia cells. Apparently leukemia cells are good at hiding - especially with the 4/11 translocation that he has, so I emphasize, NO leukemia cells anywhere in his body. Please visualize his own cells be strong, his bone marrow strong and healthy. As Ginny once said, " if we die - we win, if we live we win", but I am not ready to give up yet, I don't know how I still feel so much hope for him, but I do. Chi is beyond any sickness. If we can fill him with enough pure energy then there will be no room left for anything that is out of balance.
You are all giving us strength and I thank each one of you."

Steven from Malaysia requested a photograph of Alex be posted on the internet, so people could visualize him more easily. My sister in England read that message and used a photo of him before he was sick which she emailed to my brother in Georgia. Patrick knew how to set up a web page and in less than two hours, a photo of Alex was posted. Joel, also from Malaysia, sent us an email.

"I received the photo of Alex, thanks to Sally and Bill. Rest assured, we will continue to send specific healing chi to Alex. By coincidence, a special meeting of qigong teachers is being called tomorrow. I will make a special request to our president to send healing chi to Alex. I shall bring along Alex's photo which would definitely be of great help for visualization.

With so much love and healing chi from so many,
Alex be well,
Hao La, Joel and all the Teachers from Penang."

I knew "coincidences" are far more than that; they are the mathematics of how things work. This "higher" mathematics always works whether we see it or not, but when we are clearly aware of it, seeing signs everywhere, we know we are in harmony. The internet, making the world smaller, bringing us together, can be a powerful tool.

At the end of the day after learning Alex had the 4/11 translocation and while all this chi and love was pouring in, I went to the healing garden to pray. In a deep, tearful prayer, I told God, "If you want him, then you have to love him more than I do."

I heard three specific messages, "He's not dead yet." "Have hope." "Don't give up." It came clearly to me while he is still breathing, there is hope, and I headed back upstairs.

That night, I realized it was not me OR God, it was me AND God: God and I were parents to Alex. As I lay on the cot, beside him, I felt a huge energy in my womb. It was as if a life had been conceived by Spirit inside of me. All the energy, the prayer, all the positive thoughts, (however they were expressed,) from so many people focused on my son, gathered in my womb. My hands became hot, extremely hot, and I knew I must give this energy to Alex. I stood over his sleeping form, emitting chi to his body. I held my hands over him gently allowing the chi to flood into all of his being.

When I could tell he was full there was still heat in my hands and I visualized a little girl in the same ward. Naomi was about three years old, also with leukemia. I visualized all her tumors dissolved. Alex and Naomi are the only two children still alive from that time on the children's cancer ward.

Oliver called again about three days later. He told me, "Whatever happened between you and God, something has changed for Alex." I could see it in Alex's face and in his whole being. There was vitality in him, where before there had been none.

MAGIC MOMENTS

Once, following the chemotherapy, Alex had a reaction to the platelet transfusion. He was covered with hives, the itching intense and he was panicking. He screamed at me to get away from him, shoving me away when I tried to comfort him; he wouldn't let anyone close. We all stood helplessly while the nurses gave him benadryl, hoping to eliminate the reaction. The more upset he became, the more his nose bled, but he wouldn't let me close to wipe it. It was unbearable not being able to comfort him.

Finally, the hive-reaction stopped and he calmed down. However, the platelets hadn't taken, they hadn't been assimilated into his body and he needed yet another transfusion. The new batch took a long time to arrive.

It being 1:30 in the morning, Eric and the kids had gone back to sleep leaving the two of us. Alex's body accepted this batch without a reaction, but he was still suffering from major anxiety with more nosebleeds; so the nurses gave him some adavan to calm him. It was supposed to make him sleep, but with Alex it had an adverse reaction, he was eased somewhat, but was wide awake. I was exhausted, totally spent, but somehow love makes it possible to go beyond our physical limits.

I filled a bowl with soapy water to gently wash the blood off his hands and he began to play with the bubbles. At first I tried to do the Mom thing and enhance the moment saying, "Look at the rainbows in the bubbles," but he said, "Hush Mommy," and I stopped talking. Gradually, after a little while, I put my hands in the water and made bubbles with him, in silence, just being there. Finally as we came into harmony, things became very still. All "thought" left while in the quiet presence of timelessness, he allowed me to merge my bubble into his.

There are magic moments even in the greatest suffering when we allow them. Some moments we just survive, but then, when we allow ourselves to quiet our minds, in that moment there is magic.

I wanted Alex to *see* the chi being sent to him, I wanted it to be visual, so he could understand the level of support and love. I asked Eric to buy a map of the world, and red thread so we could put red prayer strings from wherever the chi, prayer and love was being sent. This was powerful and I asked people to tell me where they were from on the forum. Messages came from British Columbia; Penang, Malaysia; Sabah, Malaysia; Columbus, Ohio (many students); Whittier, California (and practitioners all over Orange County); Hawaii; Knoxville, Tennessee; Germany; England; Holland; Peru; Atlanta, Georgia; Indiana; Santa Fe, New Mexico; New York City; the Navajo Reservation, Tucson; Prescott, Arizona and of course China. This was only the beginning; by the end, virtually every state was represented on that map and every continent (apart from Antarctica). The ball of strings where it all came together over Alex in Phoenix, was fat; representing the sphere of chi that was protecting him.

People of every religion were represented: the love of my sister who considered herself atheist, a "born again" Christian friend from Idaho, Buddhist, Jewish, Muslim, Taoist, Hindu. More and more people sent energy and love in whatever way related to them; chi, love, prayers, positive thoughts, I gratefully accepted it all.

Another message went out when we finally returned home:

166

"Dear friends,

Thank you all once again for your amazing response concerning our son. I am sorry I could not reply earlier - internet access was hard in the hospital; but we are home now. His blood counts came back positive, cells are normal. A bone marrow test is scheduled for next Tuesday to determine if the leukemia is in remission. From that point, the key is to keep him there. As I said before, the cells can hide and then recur. With the 4/11 translocation of the cells the doctors believe that this is a certainty, but they don't know the power of chi.

I had an amazing experience in the hospital when I felt things shift for him, but I ask you all to please continue to keep him in the chi field. I take things day by day, more accurately, moment by moment. Our family is so grateful for each moment with this precious boy. Today was a good day, he has more energy by the hour and is playing with his brothers and sister quite normally. He just 'feels' healthier.

My deepest gratitude to all of you. My utmost thanks to Luke who called me in the hospital at just the right moment. Thank you for helping me to see a true reality and giving me back hope.

Please continue to send Alex love, compassion and chi. There are many red strings on our map now and Alex can visualize all the positive energy coming to him,

Thank you again and again."

Chapter 32

TOUGH DECISON

Alex did go into remission (what else could happen with so many people visualizing the same way?) There were no leukemia cells left. The question now arose, did we move forward with chi or continue medically? Now in remission, would chi be enough to keep it clear? It was heart wrenching and Eric and I both knew we could not make the decision on our own - it was just too heavy.

For a while, it looked as if we would be forced us to do the transplant. If this seemed absolutely wrong we would have fought it. I know God works through harmony, and I wanted harmony between the doctor and us, on whatever decision was made. I have to stress here that the doctors were compassionate, caring deeply for Alex, but ultimately I felt the decision should be ours.

I connected with several people, asking them to send prayer for the best choice to come clear, I also asked them to pray (or send chi) for harmony between us and the doctor. I called Luke, Oliver, Jane and a couple, David and Taco who channel spirit, all people whom I trusted on a spiritual level. I knew these prayers would be answered. In my mind the transplant was unnecessary, but that was not the outcome. It came clear the medical route was the way to go, all advice was in agreement.

The message that came through the couple that channeled for us was intense yet clear:

"Heavenly Father knows that we are in a very serious situation, but He cannot make the decision for us. That is up to us and the people involved. Physical life is so precious that we should try anything we can to sustain life.

If we do have to prepare for spirit world, then the people on Earth will feel a loneliness. If he does have to go, then offer him to spiritual world. Father sees the soul. The minute after he gets there, he will feel surrounded by love and he will feel even closer to us on Earth. Try to imagine how this will be for him; it is not something completely sad or tragic.

Rev. Moon is correct in saying that when you give someone to spirit world you should not grieve - holding on makes it harder for the person going to spirit world. Trust that he will go to a very good place. All the healing energy being given to your son at this time means that Alex is the recipient and therefore he will be elevated to a very good place.

Don't worry because he suffers in a physical sense, that memory will erase very quickly once he is in spirit world. It is VERY important to have a clear perception of how he will be in spirit world.

Right now try to set the right circumstances so he will recover. That is our first concern. Heavenly Father can prepare a greater place in eternity for him.

This kind of event will yield extra opportunity for the quality of your mission, the deepening of heart will greatly enhance your healing work. When Alex sees this from Spirit World, he will agree and he will be happy because of what he has brought to your life.

Don't give in to a tragic way of thinking."

I called Frank soon after we made the decision to go ahead with the transplant. I knew intellectually it was the "right" decision, but I had not fully united with it. Frank - who is like a wise Chinese sage - told me once you make a decision, do not go back on it. Make the best decision you can and then trust yourself. Never second guess your choice. I have since applied this advice to many other aspects of my life.

Luke advised me to ask Alex what he thought, what was *his* choice? Because he was so young, this hadn't occurred to me. Alex responded, "though it would be hard, if it would help me to live I want to do it." "I want to live." he declared. When Luke knew it was Alex's *own* desire to live, he pulled out all the stops, emailing his list of thousands asking for chi to be sent to Alex. He put a beautiful, moving message in the forum:

"Some of you probably know that Deborah Lucas's son, Alex, age 7, has been fighting Leukemia. I have interviewed at least three or four people, who survived their leukemia, despite what the doctors told them, telling their tales many years later. It is very possible that Alex will survive this ordeal.

But it is easier for us to say as we are not facing this challenge. Yet in the middle of this battle, Deborah has again and again showed us her unshaken belief in chi while she, like any other mother, uses all medical tools available for her son's recovery.

Deborah's act of love and compassion (not just because Alex is her son) toward another human being is beyond words. I am really moved. Not once, but many, many times her faith in action continues.

Now, this issue is beyond Alex as we all learn to heal and to love another individual in need. Several years ago, a little girl fell into a well in Texas, she captured the attention of the world with the whole world coming to her rescue. So I am asking you, on behalf of Deborah and her family, to make an all out effort to send chi to Alex. Spontaneous healing does occur and the more effort we put in, the better the chance.

No matter what may come out of this challenge, we all will come out better as people and stronger as a group. I have put Alex's picture on our front page internet. Please see Alex and send your love to him. We need you and your friends' help. Please put a message on our forum to show our support.

And Deborah, I can assure you, you are not alone. We are with you. Ten million Chi Lel practitioners are surrounding Alex, sending him love and compassion until he returns to your loving hands in full life force. Wan Yuan Ling Tong!

HaoLa! HaoLa!! HaoLa!!!
Luke Chan"

More and more red strings were added to our map. The support and palpable energy surrounding him intensified. Luke, now in China, took Alex's picture to the healers in the hospital there. There was an obvious shift in the energy. One healer - Jin Lao Shi was especially instrumental. He had worked before with leukemia and he ran chi, long distance, continually through Alex, scanning through his bone marrow.

Dr. Singer went to a medical conference where she happened to turn around and right in front of her was a poster of 4/11 kids, all of whom had survived. Dr. Singer learned there must be more chemo and then the child should be rushed to a bone marrow transplant, quickly, before the cancer could recur. Alex needed yet another round of chemo therapy to make sure the cancer cells didn't re-emerge. Upon successfully completing this, a perfect bone marrow match from one of his siblings was needed.

We were done with the first round of chemotherapy by December 22$^{nd.}$ Before his counts dropped to zero leading to re-hospitalized we were able to be home for a full moon qigong practice and incredibly, we remained at home through Christmas. On Christmas Eve we received a call from Dr. Singer telling us that two of Alex's brothers (Stephen and Galen) were perfect bone marrow matches.

This message was posted on the Chi-Lel forum:

"Once again, my deepest gratitude to you all. We left the hospital on Wednesday afternoon and so were able to do the full moon Chi-Lel at home. Wow! There was a HUGE amount of Chi here. I wish you could all see the way that Alex bounces back after going through even heavy chemo, his joy and lightness of heart are tremendous. Things seem to be turning around for him even medically. His chances are much greater. Two of his brothers are bone marrow matches so we are going forward with the procedure. I know the chi will keep his body strong enough to withstand a transplant with minimum side effects. Chi can also rejuvenate his body in areas that could be damaged, so it is far less scary.

The decision to continue was hard, but it became clear on every level it is the correct one, and since we came to this decision even the medical statistics are changing in his favor. I have the greatest hope the year 2000 will bring back a healthy boy.

It will be difficult - on Monday we return to the hospital where again his blood counts will drop to zero, we will be there for at least another month. But last time, the counts came back quickly. Then we travel to Tucson for the transplant...........

His family can be with him, I can stay in the same hospital room as I do in the Phoenix hospital. I am truly honored to be the mother of Alex. The other day he said, "I'm not going to die, not with my luck." We had not talked about that possibility as he needed all his strength to fight. But he came out with it anyway. He feels lucky, surrounded with love constantly and he gratefully accepts all the chi being sent to him. He knows the difference that chi makes, he feels it clearly.

Thank you for your continued love and support - it means everything to us."

Around Christmas, as I was picking up Quinn from Tae Kwon Do, I bumped into two friends, Kevin and Amy. I hadn't seen Amy for a while and I tearfully shared what had transpired since I last saw her. She asked if I could give her a photo of Alex, so she and Kevin could take it to Irma, a woman they knew in Phoenix who studied with the Tibetans. Irma is acknowledged as a high level healer by both the Tibetans and by the Hopi.

When Irma saw his picture, she reacted in a way they had never seen before. She tearfully put his picture on her altar and prayed deeply. She also gave him a pendant to wear around his neck which had a picture of the Karmapa on one side and a picture of the deity he represents on the other. The first time Alex held this gift, his headache disappeared. He learned to hold the pendant often, knowing his pain would lessen when he did.

I took Alex's photograph to the local Tibetan store to ask if they could please pass it on to Garchen Rimpoche. But it was better than that and I was told, "Oh! You have very good karma". Garchen Rimpoche was supposed to have left the day before, but his flight had been delayed and he was not leaving until the next morning. The woman from the store offered to accompany me so I could meet with Garchen personally and ask for his blessing.

We drove to Groom Creek and I was able to have an audience with him. He was a kind, unassuming man, his eyes radiating the warmth and love I felt before from Tibetan people. I know the prayers of the Tibetan monks are similar to those of the native people; they take on suffering so others don't have to. I was honored to meet with this particular Lama who endured untold suffering in his own life and maintained a totally forgiving and pure heart.

I told him about Alex, that he was VERY sick, so sick he could die. He gave me some blessings to give to

174

Alex; small brown pills, some to keep and some to put in water to drink. He gave me a mantra "Ohm, tare, tutare ture swaha," which invokes Tara (goddess of compassion). He also gave a blessing to put over the doorway. This would free anyone who walked under it from a thousand years of indemnity. This sign was placed over the hospital room door at Phoenix Children's Hospital and then at Tucson Medical Center and is now over our door at home.

I returned to the Tibetan store to buy Alex a case for the precious blessings he had been given, also to thank them again for facilitating my meeting with Garchen Rimpoche. I found a silver container designed to hold blessings around the neck that was perfect; it had an image of the Tibetan eyes on it. "That is from Swayambu, the monkey temple," I was told. I knew this was the one for Alex as Swayambu was the temple I visited in Nepal so many years before when the monks helped me through my own confusion and doubts. Now, the same connection was here to help my son.

On December 24th we received the best Christmas present we could hope for and I posted this note to the forum:

"We just heard from Alex's doctor that the DNA test on his bone marrow was completely clear. There was no sign of leukemia cells or the 4/11 translocation in his cells. This means that the transplant has a very good chance of eliminating the leukemia permanently. With so many people all visualizing ALL leukemia cells gone, how could there be any left?

The doctors feel that if we don't proceed, the leukemia will definitely return, but so many obstacles are being removed for Alex. Through chi, he is in strong remission which was very difficult to achieve. The chances that looked so small a while ago are becoming better and better. Statistically, his chances have gone from almost zero to 60%. Thank you for helping to change this outlook. Please stay with us and keep Alex strong in the chi field until he is a normal, healthy boy again."

It looked as though our family would be separated for the New Year, as Kim (who was only 9) was not allowed in the hospital due to winter restrictions for infection prevention. Again a miracle happened, Alex's counts didn't drop as quickly as predicted and we were able to go home to Prescott. On December 31st 1999 we drove home undaunted by all the crazy traffic trying to get out of the city to avoid Y2K.

We celebrated New Years together bringing in the millennium with a deep prayer. "I pray this new millennium brings us all unity and peace so we may all move into a world of health and oneness. I pray that each person reach their true potential and find true happiness."

The next morning upon awakening, we were greeted with a pure new covering of snow. I felt great hope for a pure new beginning for us all.

TUCSON

The doctors try their best to warn you how hard a transplant can be, that nothing can prepare you. This is an accurate statement.

Luke asked me to keep sending detailed messages to the forum, so people could be united in their visualization. I sent a long message before we went to Tucson, knowing it might be hard to access the internet once there.

Dear friends,
Tomorrow, we are heading down to Tucson for Alex's bone marrow transplant. I wanted to share the schedule and to ask for specific visualizations for him during this time. Chi has made a huge difference in him - he is the most positive, joyful little guy who is now helping us get through this! He is full of chi and it radiates out of him. Please help to keep chi around him during this next stage. Part of me wishes we didn't have to do this, but it is confirmed over and over again from every source it is the right thing to do.
Monday1/31/00 Out-patient surgery to insert a hickman line (instead of IV's).

Chi was already working, he had a three inch bruise under the skin, from this procedure but the next day when the dressing was changed, the bruise had completely disappeared! The nurse couldn't believe it.

The days counted down from minus 10 to day 0, the day of the transplant.

Tuesday   2/01/00   day -10   Rest
Wednesday   2/02/00   day -9   Hospital Admission
Thursday   2/03/00   day -8   Total   body   irradiation
morning and evening.   The radiation is half the usual
amount given which minimizes side effects, but some are
still possible, please use chi to protect him.   Please
visualize a) he tolerates the TBI well with minimal nausea,
b) there are no more leukemia cells, c) protection for his
sperm, d) that he be calm and not experience any fear.

I played the chi field chant during the radiation treatment. I focused on loving energy and visualized the radiation as pure, gentle chi, only bringing good into Alex's body. I couldn't be in the room with him, but I watched through the window and saw him lying calmly, without fear.

Friday   2/04/00   day -7   TBI again morning and
evening.

I worked really hard to not hate that radiation, I knew I had to turn it into loving energy.

Saturday   2/05/00   day -6   Rest
Sunday   2/06/00   day - 5   VP-16 (chemo therapy).
Please visualize there be no nausea, no drop in blood
pressure; also that the chemo find all the leukemia cells.
Monday   2/07/00   day -4   Rest, but as his counts
drop he could feel worse and worse. He could get mouth
sores, also his throat and digestive tract could become
extremely sore.   This could continue until 21 days after
transplant)

He didn't have any sores yet, but they started to develop over the next few days as the fast growing cells of his body started to break down.

Tuesday   *2/08/00*   *day -3*   *Rest*
Wednesday   *2/09/00*   *day -2*   *Melphalan, a chemo that can cause more severe nausea and vomiting.*
Thursday   *2/10/00*   *day -1*   *Rest*
Friday   *2/11/00 day -0*   *Infusion of stem cells from his brother, Galen. Please visualize that Galen gets a good harvest with plenty of stem cells and that the collection goes well.*

Galen produced a HUGE amount of stem cells.

"They hook him up to a machine and extract the stem cells from his blood. He has to endure a series of shots for a couple of weeks before the harvest to build up extra stem cells then the blood is taken from one arm, through the machine and then back into the vein in the other arm. His entire blood supply circulates through the machine three times in all in order to acquire enough stem cells, taking about four hours. Please send chi to help him tolerate the procedure."

The profound level of support continued. Red strings being added continually created a massive ball. The strings inspired Dr. Graham, the pediatric transplant doctor; he wanted to know the origin of each. I loved sharing how one came from Cornwall and another from Nepal, how we had received a message about monks from Bodnath Temple (a Tibetan Temple in Kathmandu). They heard of Alex's illness and performed a ceremony for his healing on the day of transplant.

Chapter 33

Seeing the level of excruciating pain as Alex's cells were killed was almost unbearable. He needed a shower each day and to do so he had to be aroused from his semi-conscious state. Once he was finally in the shower though, he sat in a place of bliss, warm water gently soothing him.

It was amazing to look at him as he lay on the hospital bed, tubes from several different pumps entering his fragile-looking body, seeing the miracle, the absolute bliss emanating from his face. He looked like a newborn child, just as innocent and just as close to Spirit. One day he woke suddenly out of this place of semi-consciousness, sat up and declared, "The bear is here, he is telling me to be strong"

I practiced Chi-Lel every day, usually with tears pouring from my eyes, letting myself be washed of the horror so I could face the next day anew. Luke was still in China and energy was coming directly from the hospital there. The last day of our hospital stay, during Alex's final four hour long shower, absolute peace surrounded him.

The prayers of the Tibetans and the energy from the Chinese were both working together to help Alex. In this young boy, just seven years old, China and Tibet were united.

ALEXANDER

E ven with all the miracles and the fact that Alex was still alive, the journey of his healing was not yet finished. Over the next six years he had two bouts of intense rejection.

It was exciting a year after transplant when Alex looked stable. The doses of medicine lowered and his health steadily improved, his energy rising. I anticipated a time with no medication, healing complete. However, when the dose of anti-rejection medicine dropped below a certain level, his liver counts showed his liver was not functioning properly. The counts went high, VERY high, showing the potential for permanent damage. His skin developed a darkening rash.

I gave him an abundance of chi energy. Invoking the chi field, Jesus, the Tibetans - all the help I could muster - I didn't think to protect myself and I gave him my own chi as well as directing universal chi. When practicing Chi Lel you are protected from giving your own chi if you follow certain guidelines but this concept didn't even occur to me. I just wanted him well. I gave everything I could.

The rejection stabilized, I continued giving him chi, but I was drained. When the rejection came back, I felt I failed him. I had to go extremely deep, to find places of strength. I was tired and depleted.

THE SNAKE DREAM & TONGLEN

The dream was vivid. I pulled out my intestines and digging deep into my gut found a white snake. I pulled out the snake even though I heard a voice telling me this was not a good idea, I pulled it all the way out and smashed it in the head with the base of an empty bucket until it was dead.

It was clearly symbolic but I didn't have a clue what it meant. The fact it was a snake didn't bother me; the fact it was white somehow disturbed me deeply. I borrowed my daughter's book of dream interpretations knowing I needed to grasp the meaning. As I researched, the dream became even more disturbing; the snake represented spiritual growth and awareness. "Never be scared of a snake," the book informed me. The fact it was white represented my purest Christ consciousness - and I had pulled it out, smashing it until dead.

The next three days were deeply reflective. I had been trying to escape from the overwhelming sorrow I felt. I wanted respite from the sadness. Did I really want my spiritual awareness and inner guidance to leave? - something I devoted myself to since I was seventeen.

As I was opening up, my sensitivity towards others developed, I was more in touch with the sadness of others. The week before, waves and waves of sorrow had been washing through me and I wanted to be rid of it, but now I realized I had to embrace it.

Throughout my life, how often had I been unconscious of God? And yet always, always, Spirit was with me. Now it was my turn - to consciously make the choice - do I want this course, this way of walking my life or not? I made this choice many times before, and here it was presented to me again, at a time when my heart was enveloped in almost unbearable pain. Yes, of course I was willing to keep going forward for Spirit.

Soon after this dream, I was introduced to the practice of Tonglen, a Tibetan practice of compassion. A friend, Trevor, was working with me and told me to breathe in the dark and breathe out the light. At first, while I was experiencing such levels of overwhelming sadness, I could hardly breathe at all, let alone deeply; but as my breath loosened I experienced a shift.

My friend said gently, "Remember, you are not alone in your suffering." It took me a while to realize how arrogant it was to think I was the only one to suffer, but as I began to break down my solitary barrier, I understood compassion for others in a different way.

I connected with all the other mothers in pain caused by their suffering children: mothers in Turkey who had experienced an earthquake and had tried desperately to pull their children out of the rubble; mothers in Africa who had to watch their children die of starvation or AIDS. Unable to do anything but watch the slow decline of those little ones they loved. I connected with them; *felt* their pain as my own pain.

In a deep prayer at the Tibetan Temple I pleaded, "I want to feel joy". "I have felt all this pain, now I want to know the feeling of deep joy." From the core of my being I heard, "It is the same thing."

Part Three

"Self is a sea boundless and measureless.

Say not, 'I have found the truth,'

but rather 'I have found a truth.'

Say not, 'I have found the path of the soul.'

Say rather, 'I have met the soul

walking upon my path.'

For the soul walks upon all paths.

The soul walks not upon a line,

neither does it grow like a reed.

The soul unfolds itself,

like a lotus of countless petals"

Kahlil Gibran

SUNRISE CEREMONY

It was cold in the early morning as we eagerly awaited the sun's appearance, gathered to welcome the day in the ancient tradition of the Huichol people. We were to be guided in the ceremony by a medicine man, Filipe. I had no idea what to expect. Each of us came with our own prayer and intentions united in ceremony.

I brought a photograph of my Dad who was close to leaving this earth; my prayer for him being that he would have a clear passing into spirit. I was concerned about him as he still considered himself to be an atheist. I knew I would not be with him physically at his crossing as I had been with my Mum. I gave his photograph to Filipe who reverently placed it on the altar. The site used was called Deer Valley. To the Huichol people, the deer and the medicine are one and the same; it is the deer that brings the ancient energy. It is the deer who brings the harmony we came to experience.

Filipe used his drum and eagle bone whistle to bring in the four directions and Mother Earth, summoning those who came before us. The atmosphere stilled, the connectedness deepening as each direction was beckoned. My eyes were closed; sounds, movement and smells fading as the energy enveloped me. Filipe came over and cleansed me with his eagle feathers. He gently placed one hand on my head, the other over my stomach. "You are with your father now," he said, "Be with him as when you were a little girl." Instantly, I felt myself sitting on my father's lap.

All I felt for my Dad was love and gratitude. I visualized a connection between him and my mother; saw them when they first spied each other, eye to eye in a crowded cafeteria, he an imposing 6 foot two, she slight and tiny.

Upon returning to this physical world, the sun was just peeking over the horizon, everyone standing in reverent silence. As the sun rose higher the people gathered joyfully, played instruments and danced in celebration. Drums, Tibetan bowls, the eagle bone whistle were all being played, even a distant train whistle joined in.

Filipe handed me a large round drum; I never played a drum before, but this was not a time for holding back. As my hands pounded on the drum skin it seemed to gain a life and energy of its own. An ancient Celtic rhythm came out taking me back generations. The love I experienced with my Dad reached back through our Celtic ancestry. I knew the pain that had taken place between us had healed. Any unfinished business concerning Dad and I (which had first been shown to me while in Eastern Nepal) was now accomplished, we had done it.

Filipe told me I would see Dad again. I said, "I don't think so," but he reiterated, more assertively this time, "You *will* see him again." I had already visited England twice that year. The first time in January, before he knew he was dying; this visit had brought the realization he didn't have any "stuff" left. Being eighty eight years old and blind, he had rid himself of a lot of baggage; I knew any old emotional stuff was mine, not his. I used my many hours awake due to jet lag to clear it out. That was the first time I truly respected my Dad. I saw what a wonderful person he was, a true gentleman. I valued what it must have taken for him to be communist, I admired him for that. I also understood just how deep his heart was, he accepted me and loved me no matter what my own personal choices had been.

My second visit to England had been soon after he discovered he had cancer, given six weeks to live. This presented another opportunity to clean out old stuff, especially concerning my relationship with my siblings. I seriously doubted a third meeting would occur, medicine man or not!

In August, the opportunity manifested. Dad was still alive and I was privileged to spend one more day with him. A day neither of us thought would happen, a day we both knew as a precious gift. I spoke to Dad about the sunrise ceremony, the prayer sent in his honor via the shaman. Somehow he accepted this without question; Native spirituality being easier for him to accept than standard religion.

I told him Filipe taught us how to hug, how to release a hug very, very slowly so on some level you did not separate. Dad and I continued our visit, appreciating every moment: some time spent in conversation and some merely in silence. Dad napped on and off as he grew weary and I appreciated the gentle, rhythmic sound of his breathing.

I wanted him to accept the possibility there could be more than just 'nothing' when you died. I had no agenda as to what that would be, just there may be *something*. I was reassured when he said, "No experience is lost on a writer." I knew he was open to whatever may come. Inevitably, the time came for me to leave. Both of us knew this "goodbye" was the last we would share.

He walked me to the door, stopped, gently embraced me in a last hug and released me ever so slowly, just as we had talked about. Upon separating he looked at me kindly, his blind eyes carrying so much love in them and said, "There you go."

THE ONLY CONSTANT IS CHANGE

The day after my Dad passed into spirit (which was not until mid-December, 2004), my husband told me he loved another woman. Two weeks later, he was gone, abandoning his young son, who was still in treatment for rejection from the transplant, along with his five other children, (one of whom had also contracted cancer.)

My concepts of what I thought my life was shattered. My understanding of reality dissolved. I told Spirit there were only two men I trusted, Yogananda and Thich Nhat Hanh.

Yogananda came to me in spirit. I confronted him as an equal, as a man. "Why?" I demanded to know, "Why had I been with this man, Eric? Why had he, Yogananda, directed me to join the Unification Church?" I told him "I had you already, now you are back, so what was all that about? Why? Why?" The reply came clearly, swiftly, "You needed to grow your heart."

I always believed Eric and I would transcend the confusion of this world together. I made a commitment not just to him, but to God. But, we all have choice. We can either face the dark inside us - look at it directly and accept it and then look deeper to find that all we truly are is good, beautiful and whole; or we can run. Sometimes the dark looks so terrible we try to escape it, it is almost unbearable. If we face it, suddenly those facets of ourselves that are ugly - jealousy, anger, fear, addiction to martyrdom, - they are no longer so huge and overwhelming. Instead of prohibiting our view, we can stand on them, take in a larger view. Eric chose to run. I am grateful for our time together, but more grateful he left. I was able to reclaim who I am, healing the devastating hurt. It took me nearly three years to comprehend how Eric did the honorable thing in leaving. He knew he was hurting those around him and his departure truly was the "righteous" thing to do; the only thing he could do. He was right to leave.

As my heart blasted apart, it expanded into limitless possibilities. From my confusion a prayer went out. I said to the universe, "You have to help, I didn't ask for this, this is too much for any one person to carry." I walked around my property and prayed, "This place is too much for me; it needs to be a healing place." My prayer was received - my prayer (based on my son's miraculous healing) was for each person visiting my center to receive the healing they needed, even if they only came for coffee. Amazing things opened up. Along with the healing others found, I was given the gift of my own healing, understanding the blessings behind the wounds of my life. I found my heart path.

I searched within myself, discovering my strength. "My God! I am so strong," blasted into my mind. The other immediate experience was liberation, I felt so free. This surprised me, leaving me feeling guilty. Those were the truthful flashes of the situation but I was also extremely disoriented; I had given so much to my marriage. I had been absolutely committed; it had lasted 27 years (more than half my life). I began to see how much I had given up in that time, how much I had compromised. I took back the name Daisy. I had travelled to India and to America, on my own with that name, it gave me great strength to reclaim it.

I was acutely aware that the patterns I needed to shift not only came from the last twenty-seven years but also from my culture, how I was raised. I knew they went deeper still. There were patterns established before I was born. How many patterns connected to Spirit, how many being valuable for my highest good? As I looked, it became brutally apparent - not much. I began eliminating patterns that no longer served me. At first, I thought it couldn't be too hard; however, soon the tsunami of change challenged me to the core.

It was as if I were in a cocoon, dark and alone. When a butterfly is in a cocoon, all the cells are re-arranged and re-structured. It was an uncomfortable place, old patterns dropped, shifted and re-aligned.

I knew I needed to do something to enable me to shift faster. For me to make it financially I would have needed to get two jobs, no longer home-schooling and rarely seeing my children. I told Spirit there had to be another solution. It was *not* acceptable my children lose not just their father, but also their mother. Cleaning vacation homes was one venture but I spent more on car repairs than I earned. My financial world was just one reflection of my own confusion; I didn't know how to make all of this work. The universe had to help me. I knew I was not alone; I felt tremendous support both from Spirit and from Earth.

Throughout my life's journey I didn't look back and didn't think much about old friends. Even so, someone from my past, Lisa, felt something was wrong. It had been thirty years since we last talked, but she knew I needed help. Lisa told her husband, Hugh, "Something is wrong with Daisy, we have to find her." They googled me on the internet and I received an email asking, "Is everything alright love?" in true Cornish style. These two people gave me a strong message. They let me know all is O.K. They let me know it was all much bigger, working as planned. I came to terms with the fact that I knew nothing; I had to discard all previously accumulated life's knowledge concerning reality and you know? – A tremendous weight lifted. It is not a bad place to begin, to know absolutely nothing.

Yogananda continually visited, comforting me through spirit. The community of Prescott swept me up. Through each melt-down, the right person turned up giving what I needed, be it a hug or much needed insight. I was never alone, truly knowing love and support. The time came when I was strong enough to take a step for myself. It came crystal clear that I needed to go to China to study more Qigong with Luke.

CHINA

On the ferry-ride from Hong Kong to ZhongShan, I looked around the sea of Chinese faces. Each had a brilliant light, which merged into one light containing all of us. We were all part of the same energy field and I was awed by the sight of it. Luke greeted me in ZhongShan, China, with the enthusiastic words, "We are all one." He said it as if he was experiencing it, right then, not as something read and then repeated.

Luke was inspired; he was currently translating the Tao Te Ching. He was adjusting his chi gong method as the practical part of Lao Tse's teachings. I was amazed what Luke had learned and integrated in the few years since our last meeting. Luke, who had previously dismissed prayer, and taught Chi Lel only as a healing art, was now taking his understanding much deeper and incorporating meditation as a way for us to evolve and reach our potential as human beings.

The air was thick and humid though fortunately not too hot. It was July, I had been warned not to go to Southern China in summer, but what can you do? The right time is the right time!

The first thing Luke did was take me to a local restaurant; wanting me to have a taste of China and dive into my experience completely. Everything was alive, waiting to be cooked – frogs, shrimp, crabs, eels, cat fish, baby pigeons, big black beetles. There was also a wonderful selection of fresh vegetables.

It was a funky outdoor restaurant, with excellent food. ZhongShan is beautiful and lush, reminiscent of Hawaii. Before arriving at Luke's apartment complex he bought fresh lychee and dragon fruit from a road stand. My first bite of lychee informed me I had tasted heaven. It was unlike anything I had eaten before, sweet and juicy, yet subtle and delicate. Each succulent mouthful was worth every second of July heat.

In the evening, Luke treated me to the first of many massages, I was confused when the young Chinese masseuses all started giggling at something Luke said in Chinese. Great amusement on their faces, they all turned to look at me. All were girls, except one young man, Fu. Luke had apparently told them I was now single and Fu should come back to America with me! Luke in his wisdom knew that I needed to be flattered by a man, even if it was just a game. They were vibrant, happy people, regularly bursting into fits of giggles as they tried to teach us Chinese. The foot massages were relaxing after so much Qigong. Luke has four students at a time in China, so there were five of us in a row getting massages at the same time.

Everything was different, the tastes, the smells, the atmosphere, the sounds, the language; it is one reason I love to travel. As I lay in bed my first night, I was struck by how nothing was familiar. It was wonderful to be in a different country again, content and relaxed

Dawn woke me early and I took a walk in the lush grounds by a man-made lake. Finding a spot on the lake's bank then another in a little gazebo also by the water, I created prayer places for myself. I watched the fish feeding and followed the ripples from their movement across the water. Each small motion sent ripples all the way to the banks just as each thing we do affects everything. Each thought, each idea, each action sends ripples into the whole.
I returned to the same spot at dusk every evening. I took the hour to be on my own, watching the bats swoop down to the still water for a drink. The frogs were

numerous, jumping as I passed by; the more time I spent quietly by the water the more frogs I became aware of. Some were so tiny, no bigger than the finger nail of my little finger. It was a place of great peace, my thoughts and emotions clearing.

My first day off from intense Qigong training presented me the opportunity to leave the seclusion of the compound. Luke took us to breakfast. There were about twenty dishes to choose from; a mixture of sweet, spicy and savory. I had no idea what anything was, so each bite was an adventure. Luke soon realized I loved a particular sweet pastry with custard making sure I had plenty. He also made me understand it was O.K. to eat them first. It is a concept that I have since grown to love – why not have desert before dinner if you feel like it? According to Luke, there are no rules in China.

After breakfast, I ventured into town along with the other students. When the "no rules in China" concept was applied to driving it made things pretty interesting! There were scooters everywhere, cars, bicycles, trucks, taxi cabs and pedestrians each competing for right of way. Traffic signals were minimal. Our cab driver just honked his horn as he drove straight through the red light. Crosswalks for pedestrians existed but they made no difference. If there was a brief gap in the traffic, you had to run for it; there was no time for hesitation or lack of confidence.

The rains of the summer season poured and the water gathered up to my ankles. I was soaked to my knees. Umbrellas were exceptionally cheap so at least my head remained dry. We found a steep flight of steps leading from a back street and followed them up and up through lush bamboo and palm trees. Not having a clue where we were going it felt exhilarating as the rain drenched us. At the top it opened up to a clearing with an ancient pagoda.

China was not at all what I expected. I thought the people would be nice, but with an air of oppression. I was wrong; the people were friendly, bright and happy. I did not feel any oppression. There were jobs created for everyone, many stores having greeters whose sole purpose was to welcome you.

Late in the day, we met up with Lily, Luke's wife, who took us to a crowded restaurant for dinner. It was hectic and loud with dish upon dish of various foods served. I loved the lotus roots and even tried the baby pigeons, the local delicacy. They were pretty tasty, but there was not much meat and I found the head being still attached a little disconcerting.

People were loud, the servers and cooks working hard and fast to keep up with the enthusiastic crowd. It was intense; the sounds, tastes, smells and chaos completely unfamiliar to me. I found myself slowing down, my mind separating from what was taking place. I became very "present" and felt great compassion and love for each person. As I looked around, I thought of Yogananda's saying, "Let my soul smile through my heart and my heart smile through my eyes, that I may scatter rich smiles in sad hearts." From my place of observance, I had time to focus on each person.

As I lay in bed that night, playing the Tibetan CD "Ohm Mani Padme Ohm", I focused on bringing healing into my body. I slowly and consciously spun the energy in the lower dantien (the lower dantien is the energy center between the navel and the point on the spine directly opposite.) Butterflies came in, all of nature - circling my dantien, thoughts of Islam harmonizing with Christianity, all races and creeds intentionally being God-conscious;

everything existing in peace. I didn't just imagine it; I felt it and knew this reality in every cell of my body.

Meditations I experienced while in China were profound. I had taken the DVD 'What the Bleep' for Luke. He loved it, continually referring to "keeping all your basket balls bouncing," a metaphor for keeping all ones realities moving. It is so easy to limit ourselves. It was a new concept and challenge to keep *all* possibilities open, putting no limits on anything.

During one meditation I became worried and agitated. I summoned Yogananda to assist me with understanding. I felt him join me; alas it was soon obvious I couldn't quiet my "mind chatter". As Yogananda departed, I felt him push back my hair and gently kiss me saying, "You are not quite ready."

Luke made a CD of sounds for meditation and we concentrated on the tones he used. I connected with them deeply and then merged into silence. I brought chi into my lower dantien. Feeling connected, I moved the chi into the earth. From the dantien, I moved the energy up. I asked Yogananda to come and please show me which way to go to reach cosmic consciousness, to reach God. He led me to my Christ consciousness then to my crown chakra. I was able to go partly out but as the meditation concluded I knew I needed to come back to my body. I felt totally joyful, experiencing God's Spirit in each of my cells, each cell alive. Yogananda told me, "Don't worry; this feeling is not lost."

I connected to the lower dantien more deeply in meditation a couple of days later; the chanting went into an enormous, beautiful space. I brought God's love from the crown into my dantien feeling love consume my being. I wanted to develop this – to understand the relationship between the dantien and cosmic consciousness.

During the next meditation, a picture of a rotor rooter came to mind. I started to bring up the energy, birthing the thought, "no, to go up, it has to go down." Soon the energy came up on its own and I observed my central line, wide and pulsing. Everything opened up. My body and mind opened completely beyond the limitations of wonderful, powerful. After a while I reached out to my children, Alex, Kim and Quinn. One at a time I connected with them.

On the last day of my visit, I returned to Zhong Shan. This time I chose to experience it by myself. As I walked through the crowded streets, I felt completely safe. I found the Chinese to be friendly and warm. I noticed beggars, but in each case I observed, begging was the only choice for them to exist. They were respected, they were doing what they had to do. I gave money to a man with no legs who moved by riding a skate-board type contraption. I gave money to a crippled woman who was accompanied by a young blind boy. I gave gladly, yet the old conflicting shadow of Atlas' shoulders fluttered at the edge of my mind; just enough to remind me of how I used to feel. The beggars touched my heart; I gave them money and prayers now instead of exhausting confusion. Compassion became my tool of choice.

I headed to a Buddhist Temple and as I climbed the steps, there was another beggar sitting near the entrance. I looked at his eyes, the thought impacting me – "you are enlightened aren't you?" He knew *exactly* why he was there. I gave him money and continued on into the temple. Passing through the green gates, I was greeted by a raised mural of brightly painted dragons. I spent time visiting the various sections. As I was about to leave, a group of women, all dressed in black, came to worship, rebirthing the ancient intended purpose of meditation and prayer. One of the women looked at me, she began motioning me to join them in prayer. Though surprised I quickly nodded.

The women looked in my bag discovering I had purchased a beautiful, black velvet jacket. They placed it over my bare shoulders, nodding to each other in approval. Now I was dressed acceptably, I could enter the main temple filled with golden Buddhas. The women took care of me, handing me a book of chants printed in Chinese. When I held it upside down, they patiently righted it. Showing me when the chanting had reached the end of the page. They gestured for me to turn the page and showed me when to stand, to sit, to bow. I was privileged to be in their company.

I prayed deeply, knowing the connection with all the people present; first the women, also the monks. The monks were an odd mixture of ancient and modern as is the rest of China. Wearing their traditional robes they chanted into a microphone; one young monk leaving momentarily, cell phone ringing, returned with a look of embarrassment. My feeling of connectedness expanded. I prayed that as I made steps forward in my life, it would affect each person in a positive way. I prayed to walk true to my path, helping those striving to walk the best way in *their* lives. "We are one," was how Luke had greeted me when I first arrived. It had now taken on a truer, expanded meaning.

As I left, the beggar was still at the entrance. Without hesitation, I dug into my purse to give him a little more money, but he looked at me with his knowing eyes; I had given enough. I knew my heart had finally learned compassion. I wonder if that man, that precious soul, still lies at that Temple entrance, or if he only happened to be there once, exactly when I needed him.

The morning I left China, a butterfly landed on my pants and crawled upon my lowered finger. It stayed with me, gentle wings pulsating, allowing me the gift of time to find a flower I considered beautiful and perfect. I knew I had emerged from my cocoon. Interestingly, the one word I learned in Chinese from the masseuses was the word for butterfly.

OVERS

I emerged from the cocoon, but didn't know how to fly. I returned to America, inspired but immobile - I felt like a newly hatched butterfly, sitting on a branch with wet wings.

Soon after my return, I met a yoga teacher, Michael. He had recently attended a workshop with Thich Nhah Hanh and he shared a most beautiful teaching of how to have compassion towards oneself. He told me Thich Nhah Hanh had shown him how to take parts of yourself that were hurt or parts that you didn't like; to take them and hold them in your arms as you would an infant. As you hold an infant, you love it unconditionally.

I applied this to many parts of myself, holding them, comforting them, letting the insecure parts know they were loved; letting the jealous parts know they were safe; the abandoned parts know they were wanted; the angry parts I soothed. I learned to comfort and love myself. It was the first time in my life I applied the concept of actually loving *myself*; that *I* was worth loving.

My wings finally dried out, how wonderful to feel joy again! But, I didn't know how to land. I couldn't ground. I felt more comfortable in spirit reality than in this one, how could I make *this* world work? I knew from my meditations it was absolutely possible to integrate all of it, but I didn't understand how.

Some of the answer came through Filipe, the shaman I met earlier. I was impressed by the sincerity of his prayer. He said how he is nothing and no-one but he does his best to be obedient to Spirit and I believed him.

I had participated in the sunrise ceremony with him. He brought me a new language, a different way of understanding Great Spirit, an ancient native way. He introduced me to the energy of the Huichol people; people whose connection goes back thousands of years, people who have not lost their ancient knowledge.

In October, three months after my return from China, Filipe returned to Prescott and I attended another sunrise ceremony led by him. This was followed by a sweat lodge, led by a young Sundancer, Isaiah. Filipe told us, "You have entered one door, now use the sweat lodge to go through the next." Yogananda had already told me I needed someone in a physical body to help me and as I entered the sweat lodge I felt Yogananda gently leave. The intense connection I felt with him over the past nine months disipated.

There are many doorways to understanding our wholeness, who we truly are, and this is the one that opened to me at the time. Filipe helped me gain confidence to fly. He helped me ground. He helped me cut the bonds of old, restricting patterns and he helped me remember how to laugh.

Filipe asked that someone continue to visit the altar where the sunrise ceremonies had been held. He said the energy would stay as long as one person went on a regular basis. I knew this to be what I needed to do; I did it to hold the space. I viewed it as an opportunity, not an obligation. There were many mornings when I went out to the mountain to pray, sometimes it was seventeen degrees, sometimes fourteen, but I never felt cold while I in prayer. It was only later, when the sun had finally risen and I made my way back I realized how chilled I was.

When I couldn't make the long drive, I would greet the sun from my land. I prayed for the spirits to wake up on my land, for it to feel as alive as it did on the mountain.

In February 2006, a friend, Annie, came to teach a seminar about changing old patterns. She helped me touch a place of absolute beingness. I came to understand I am not my story, I am not even my spirituality. There are parts of ourselves we get attached to, that we identify with. However important they may seem, if we attach to them too densely, they stop us seeing who we truly are. Mother, teacher, writer, musician, spiritual – they are all merely labels. We are bigger than any of them.

"What about ego?" I asked her. Annie replied, "Just say thank you. All of these patterns, ego, unworthiness, jealousy, whatever they may be, were at one time useful to us, so say 'thank you, you did your job, but you are no longer needed'."

Annie showed me that the sense of connectedness I felt never leaves us; this was Yogananda's teaching. Through Filipe and the altar, I came to understand it is all we truly are.

I learned to clean out old patterns which stop me from manifesting my higher being of beauty. I had acquired many tools. I found all teachings are basically the same; they are ways for us to eliminate our limitations and step into our wholeness.

Late February, I met Filipe on the Navajo reservation. Having no idea what to expect, Spirit made it clear to me I was to go. It was important. I found I loved the reservation. There is something about the energy there that resonates with me, I feel connected. Each time I have gone, the experience has been choreographed for me by Spirit, the reservation knew I was coming. On my first visit, we happened to bump into a native elder Filipe knew. He invited us to a powwow he was organizing.

As we were driving around Gallup, Filipe said, "You called 'overs'." I didn't know what he was talking about. When he saw the questioning look on my face, he went on to explain the game of jacks. I vaguely remembered playing jacks, so I had some idea of bouncing the ball, grabbing the six-pronged little jacks and catching the ball before it hit the ground again, but I didn't remember anything about "overs". In Filipe's version of the game, if you called "overs" fast enough before anyone else could grab the pieces, you got to have another chance. "You called 'overs', you get a new chance in life," he said.

I met several of Filipe's friends. My sense of my own value was embarrassingly small but I began to look up instead of hiding in my shyness. Looking around, letting in the reservation, I was welcomed by Filipe's friends and something began to shift inside me.

The powwow was held in a school gymnasium, it had the usual wooden floor, uncomfortable tiered seating, the acoustics creating a hollow echo. *This* space was not hollow at all, it was filled with energy and color. It held a sense of purpose. The contestants danced in costumes of bright, intense colors, decorated with multitudes of feathers. Each costume obviously made with great love and pride. Reds, yellows, blues, golds, fabrics, feathers, silver ornaments all merging in movement, passion and competition, each one trying his best to outdo the others. For some, there was no competition, there was only the dance. These *became* the spirit they represented. They carried stillness and presence in their movements. They danced on the plains beyond a noisy gymnasium.

I was the only white person there. Yet in Filipe's company I didn't feel an outsider. When the young girls danced, he encouraged me to go up to them and give them money as others had done. He even gave me the money to give them, pushing me to the front. With Filipe's gentle encouragement, I began to step forward.

We didn't stay too long, he was aware when I reached a certain point and it was time to go. We walked out to the parking lot; I felt like a child, full of wonder, happy. Filipe asked me to share something about myself, "Your turn," he said. What I ended up telling him was about my time in the Himalayas, about the experience of "knowing" God, alone in the mountains, just me and Creator. It was this sense of renewal I now felt.

Filipe traded on the reservation and ended up with a whole eagle and numerous sets of feathers to do his exquisite fan work. One set of feathers was somewhat ragged; Filipe laughed saying how it looked as though it had been run over by a truck. It was a privilege and an eye-opener to see how he loved and honored those feathers. He talked to them, addressing them respectfully as "Grandpa". He told them not to worry; they would soon be showing their glory again. He joked with them, and stroked them lovingly back into shape, trimming them where needed.

I was awed by the whole scenario. Being an artist, I tend to look at faces longer than normal and I soaked up the whole experience, the light on Filipe's nose, the angle of his head as he gently worked with the feathers. I knew I wanted to draw him. My own creativity rebirthing.

Part of the eagle's tail was left, where the feathers had been removed, and Filipe planned to bury it on the reservation. But as we were driving towards Prescott, he remembered he had failed to do so. He thought of burying it in the forest outside of Flagstaff, instead he looked at me and said, "This needs to be taken to your place."

Arriving home, before doing anything else, we went outside to an area where a sweat lodge had previously been.

Filipe gently placed the part of the eagle in a large juniper tree. I love that tree; memories of javelinas giving birth; Alex climbing in it, discovering a road runner right above his head. It brings shelter to the birds and protects the rabbits that often nest among its roots. It was here Filipe brought the honoring of the eagle. He told me how it was a female eagle (he could tell by its size) and that it would bring protection to my land. I thought of my prayers wanting the spirits of my land to wake up. I knew this was an answer to my prayer.

When Filipe saw the healing center, he knew the altar belonged here. At first it was simple, cushions and a few deer skins with some hikuri medicine. Each time Filipe returned from visiting the desert in Mexico, more would arrive; beaded deer skulls, a buffalo skull which later was also beaded, Huichol chairs and more deer skins. Later he brought sacred water from the sacred springs where the Huichol do their pilgrimage.

Filipe told me the energy wanted to be there, it was a reward for my vigilance holding the space on the mountain.

Filipe compared me to the eagle feathers that he had nurtured back to beauty. How I raised my children as the eagle does on the cliff, exposed to the elements and they would never be able to look at life in a "normal" way. He told me, how, like the feathers I was a little beat up, but the beauty was not lost, the nobility still there. I listened as tears streamed down my face washing my heart.

NAVAJO HATS

My second adventure on the reservation took me to the Gallup flea market. English was not always being spoken, it was Navajo. It was exciting, reminiscent of traveling to a foreign country. Everything was for sale in the flea market, anything you could imagine, from toasters to old CD's, from hats and used clothing to flutes and colorful beaded handles.

We were hungry and stopped to get a Navajo burger. Filipe was pleased to be the first to introduce me to one of the unhealthiest items you could eat, but it tasted so good and licking the grease from your fingers made it even better. It consisted of two beef patties with tomato, lettuce and onion wrapped in wonderfully greasy fry bread. We were trying to be good and split the first one between us, but we quickly returned to buy another. We reconnected with one of Filipe's friends from our previous trip. It was a good feeling to see someone familiar and to know I was welcomed back.

One stall had paintings and hats for sale. There was one unique hat made of skin and lined with fur around the edge with turkey feathers attached to the top with red thread. I knew my son, Quinn, would love this traditional Navajo hunting hat but it was eighty dollars and I only had twenty dollars with me. I mentioned this to Filipe and he took me to his van where he had two very large turkey wings.

"Go and trade for it," he said, placing the wings in my hands. I looked at him aghast, "What, me?" This was not the only time I said, "What me?" to Filipe as he pushed me to go beyond my perceived limits. He was serious and not going to let me off easily. Filipe was enjoying himself immensely at the sight of me; a small, white woman trucking through the flea market with a humongous turkey wing in each hand.

It was an elderly Navajo man I traded with, I don't think he could believe what he was doing any more than I could, but I could see in his eyes he *really* wanted those turkey wings. He kept saying how much gas was and how he needed the money but my skills learned in the bazaars of Istanbul and Kabul and honed in the markets of Calcutta emerged quickly.

After a reasonable bargaining time, it was obvious he would not do a straight trade so I offered him the feathers *and* the twenty dollars from my pocket. His lined face split into a smile as he took my hand, shook it and declared "Good trade". The "deal" complete, he proceeded to share the meaning of his art. He explained the usage of my new hat while hunting by pointing to the examples in his paintings. He assured me how much he valued the turkey feathers and how they would be honored in his work. I returned to Filipe with a huge grin on my face, hat in hand!

It was a few days later when I realized my face was aching, my jaw hurt. I found I was smiling all the time and my muscles weren't used to it. With this thought I burst out laughing.

HOW MY SONG ~ THE FLUTE ~ AND MY ART ….. WERE ALL GIVEN BACK

As people came to the altar, Filipe began teaching me to use the energy. He handed me the drum urging me to sing a song. I definitely had the, "What me?" look on my face. He reassured me, "Don't worry, the drum will teach you, just listen." I trusted him and sure enough as I listened, I heard a song, a simple chant. It went, "Spiritus Sanctus." I had no idea what it meant, but it came clearly and I began to sing softly. The people who gathered began to sing with me. With each added voice the chant strengthened.

Filipe had seen one of my drawings from a class I had taken. He was blown away saying, "Girl, you *have* to do your art, it is part of your healing." I had not been able to draw while Alex was sick, I couldn't access my creativity. But, as he improved, I took a drawing class, waking up parts of me which had been dormant for many years. When Eric walked out, my art once again receded. Filipe encouraged me to draw but I had no clue where to begin. "Just get your tools together," he advised. I started by simply sharpening a pencil and it felt wonderful. Gradually my art woke up and quickly shifted to a level never reached before.

The altar gave me an image it wanted me to paint, Filipe's profile. It showed his relationship to the deer, how the horn of the deer pierced his skin and went behind his eye. It later came to me that the image should be on a drum head and that it should include feathers. I knew I was not ready to create it, I had much to learn. I made a simple

211

pencil drawing of Don Ramon, Filipe's teacher who was in Spirit. The first day, nothing came, I couldn't capture the image. But on the second day, I was told clearly to start with the eyes. As I did so Don Ramon came to me and started teaching me from spirit. This drawing took a long time; I continued to work on it slowly while working on several other pieces. Don Ramon taught me about the prayer in the feathers and I established a relationship with his powerful presence.

Early May, 2006, I journeyed at the altar with a group. I didn't usually journey when people were there as Filipe wanted me to study and learn from what he did; learning to facilitate for others. This time, he felt it was what I should do. As I found myself settling into a profound peace, I asked Don Ramon to teach me what I needed to know.

He came and "walked" right into me. While there, he was dancing and I felt myself dancing too; a dance of the Huichol. When he stepped out I continued to dance. In my journey I was taken to the ceremonial center. I was invited inside where many Huichol people sat. What I saw was God manifest in people. I said in awe, "There are so many of them," so many who live in absolute harmony with Creator.

I felt Spirit manifest in me and when a thought came, I followed it with Spirit and came effortlessly back to center; nothing could separate me any more. My prayer was to let God into every part of me. I felt Spirit take over. I couldn't (didn't want to) hold on to "me". I lay harmonized asking Spirit to show me what I needed to learn. He said, "I am your Creator – I run in your veins and in your DNA, there is no separation." I knew Spirit is not something "out there" but is truly inside me.

On May 20, 2006, I wrote:
> "Today, you started Kindergarten." This is what Filipe told me. I am learning to trust my intuition. I tend to see only the good in people, but I find that I need to be okay with seeing where people are on their journey, without judgment. I need to trust my gut feelings and believe in what I am doing.

My May 21st conversation with Spirit:
> Spirit reminded me, "You prayed many years ago to know My heart – this is it." "How can I do what I need to?" I asked. "Stay in the light knowing your connection to all. Stay in the light" I was told.

Late May 2006, I did another drawing, this one depicting the hicuri medicine. The medicine I chose to draw was in seven sections. Filipe told me the seven part medicine teaches seven words, telling me to listen for a new word daily for the next seven days. These words would guide me for the rest of my life. The words came clearly, sometimes early in the morning, sometimes later in the day, each one obvious.

My words were:
> Energize
>> Healing
>>> Union
>>>> Integration
>>>> Stillness
>>>>> Unfolding
>>>>>> Celebration

On the eighth day I was given one more word – delight – I knew it was a clarification of the word "celebration", Spirit knew I couldn't yet understand the level of joy implied by the word celebration.

The words continue to teach me, the same words, but understood to greater depths as my healing deepens. The union is with Great Spirit, the integration is bringing it into this life, into every breath, every action. But it is only in stillness, as I learn to quiet my busy brain and stop the cacophony of thoughts that cascade through my mind, that my life can truly unfold. From that deeper state of being where true knowledge and creativity arise, I know I am being led by Spirit.

Filipe knew how serious I tended to be. He saw how I was unable to release the heavy weight I still thought I had to carry. He supplied me with tools enabling me to begin the process of letting it go. One of the most powerful tools was simply gratitude.

He would ask me, "Can you go to the bathroom?" When I said, "Yes," he replied "Then, be grateful, some people can't". "Do you have cancer?" Filipe asked. "No" I answered. "Then be grateful. Do you have a roof over your head?" "Yes." "Then be grateful" he reiterated. "Do you have food in the refrigerator?" "Yes." "Then be grateful." This conversation with Filipe continued until all I could feel was gratitude, no room remaining for self-pity.

Filipe could always tell whether I was balanced or not. "How are you doing this morning," he would ask. One morning I replied "good" but it was far from heart felt. He asked me again, "How are you doing?" "Good," I replied again. He looked at me and said, "I feeeeeel goooood." He said it how James Brown sang it and he said it as if he *really* meant it. "O.K." he said, "Now you say it like that."

I was embarrassed, but I tried. "I feel good." Filipe looked at me as if to say, "I don't think so", so I tried again, "I feel goood." It was a little better, but still unconvincing. Filipe encouraged me, "You can do better than that, one day you will be teaching others to do this." I attempted once more, but before Filipe could say anything I looked at him, stating, "I'm not there yet am I?" It was time for me to take my daughter to school, I didn't practice on the way there with her in the car, but on the way back, when I was alone, I repeated over and over, "I feel good," until finally it came out "I feeeeeeel goooooood," and you know what? I did. I felt great!

In June, Filipe went to the Sundance, my son Alex in tow; this was where Alex had a final healing of the rejection from the transplant. I stayed in Prescott knowing this was Alex's own journey. I prayed deeply each day connecting to the Sundance in spirit. It was the drumming, day and night for ten days that finally brought Alex and the transplanted marrow from his brother into the same resonance. The drumming went deep, penetrating the bone-marrow and the rejection that had lasted for so long was finally over.

I was shown by Spirit I had to let Alex go. The hardest thing I had to face was knowing on some level I was holding on to Alex's sickness. Part of his healing required me seeing this. It was horrible to acknowledge, I saw where I believed his disease gave me value. Of course, I wasn't conscious of this, so I needed to see it now – yuck! It is so hard to look at those parts we choose to ignore. For me, the fact some of Alex's inability to completely recover was directly caused by me was sickening, but as I looked at it, I knew I had the strength to let it go. I had the strength to look it squarely in the eye, face it and set Alex free.

Filipe was still at the Sundance when two women, Sharon and Joan, came to the altar and I drummed for them. It was the first time I worked at the altar sans Filipe. As I drummed, I felt a huge distinction between my drumming and the drum, the drum provided the journey, not me. I heard notes and tones in the drum I had not noticed before. Both the women had experiences taking them as deep as when Filipe was there and Sharon told me how she heard drumming coming not just from inside the room, but from outside, connected with nature.

I loved that drum, it resonated with my voice as I sang; and I loved the eagle drumstick that beat with its own rhythm. I spent many hours using them, they relaxed and connected me, carrying my prayers. When Filipe returned and gave the drum stick away, I was devastated, I couldn't believe what he was doing and could not contain the tears that welled up. How could he give away *my* drumstick? This was the drum stick I used, that had taken me to beautiful places and brought me balance. How would I manage without it?

Filipe became quite angry with me, "These are just instruments," he said, "They go to wherever they should." He went outside, broke a stick off the nearest bush wrapping the end in leather. "*This* is your drumstick," he said abruptly. "Don't *ever* confuse the instrument with the person, it is the person beating the drum and playing the flute that makes the difference."

On June 19, 2006, my granddaughter was born at 6:45 am. I was holding her a few hours after her birth when two Navajo brothers came in. My son met them and they had promised to bring a blessing to his daughter on the day of her birth. Michael played the flute while Robert offered a beautiful blessing. Robert blew an eagle bone whistle for the first time to welcome her to this world.

They had a small flute with them, a little double flute and I asked to look at it. Michael encouraged me to blow into it; it was magic to play a flute again. Spirit

216

clearly told me to buy the flute, but it was not cheap and I hesitated. Again, the voice came loud and clear, "You need this flute, it is a gift, the money will come back to you." This time I paid attention, wrote a check and gratefully took the flute home.

At the altar, I offered the flute to Spirit. I prayed it would connect to the drum which allowed people to journey. I also prayed each time I played the flute, it would carry a prayer for my granddaughter.

A few days later, I got a call from Costco, they found a check written by me, the check written to Michael for the flute, it had somehow been dropped in one of the aisles. I had been told by Spirit the money would come back. I had to shake my head and laugh as here was the check literally back in my hand.

I began earnestly playing my new flute every day. As people journeyed with the flute music, the song constantly changed. More flutes came to me and the energy of the altar taught me how to play them, the purpose of each one and how to offer a prayer though the music. They became like the drum, it was not me playing. The flutes have a song of their own.

Chapter 41

JUST ME AND SPIRIT

Filipe returned to his home in the Mexican desert but on his way through Texas, he sent me a new eagle-bone drumstick to replace the one he had given away.

On August 4th 2006, I was singing using the drumstick for the first time. As I began to sing, a song came with words I didn't know. At first it was just sounds, but as it continued I could hear language. The song took me to a place of great harmony and I understood the oneness of Spirit and Earth. The language was ancient, before languages separated; the song sang me to a place of no separation. A black panther appeared, the animals smiled.

On August 9th 2006 I was again at the altar, once more playing the drum using the eagle bone drumstick. Again the song came with words I did not know. The deer came and directed me to follow, I was told "Come with me but we are not going to the same place we usually go."

I was told not to be afraid, and I prayed to be ready. I was reassured, "You are." I was told, "You are all aligned." I was taken to the place of peace in this world where Arabs and Jews harmonized, where black and white were friends, as I had been in China. But this time the oneness continued to expand out to the universe - an expansion of that absolute oneness and peace.

After a while, I was told to come back, clearly hearing, "You are only just beginning!" My relationship with the energy continued to deepen as did my understanding.

On one of the many mornings when I greeted the sun, I prayed about joy. I always connected to Creator as the sun rose, however as my day progressed, harmony became more difficult to maintain. I told Spirit I wanted to be joyful and connected continually. Somewhere in my subconscious disease festered. I still carried guilt, happiness eluded me. The old thought, "every other person must be happy before me" began to surface.

Spirit told me "It is your birthright to walk in the joy of Spirit. The fact that you walk this earth is enough; you are entitled to know God's love. To walk in God's love, in absolute joy, is your BIRTHRIGHT – claim it, *seize* it."

MEDICINE WOMAN

Filipe returned to Prescott early in December. He told me the deer had come to him declaring he be here for Christmas. Whenever Filipe was in town, people found out quickly. This visit was different from the previous ones, Filipe pushing me to take care of people on my own. December 13th saw the arrival of three people, one after the other.

Jackie, arrived at 7:00am. I drummed and played the flute for her while she journeyed receiving what she wanted in her prayer. I then rested for a while. Shortly another woman, Linda, came and Spirit taught me how to rebirth her. I had been praying about what the energy wanted me to do. How was the healing to take place? Was I supposed to take the sickness into me then bring energy to heal myself? It was clear that the key is rebirth. Great relief filled me.

Filipe brought some yarn paintings with him from Mexico. One I absolutely *knew* had to stay at the altar. He almost sold it to someone, but I was uncompromising and told him, "No, that one needs to stay here." I knew I needed to learn from this particular painting. It is a circular picture of a woman, legs wide open giving birth to children of different colors. There are children at the top of her head, deep in the birth canal and newly emerged from the opening. Her arms are stretched out, turning into snakes, (snakes being protectors for the Huichol.) Completely vulnerable she is undeniably protected. There is a wolf on one side with a deer on the other, both being formidable guardians, legends in their own right. Her heart is held open for her by two, what look like hands, (not her own), holding it wide open. Her heart is filled with light, as is the

221

birthing canal. Filipe had talked how women have the ability to give birth and to rebirth. The painting insisted it remain as it was my teacher.

I played the drum for Linda directing my heart to open; it was held for me as depicted in the painting. I allowed Linda to be brought into me and felt her birthed, through the birth canal. I then nurtured her. Both she and I were birthed at the same time.

Spirit then asked if I wanted to do it again for me. So, as Linda rested, I gave birth to myself through the birth canal, all of me reborn. I felt very small, as I felt years ago when I passed through the last gate at Swayambu Temple in Kathmandu. All I no longer needed was left in the shell that was no longer me; the new "me" emerged. As Linda came back from her journey, we shared for a while. Filipe came in stating to her, "This is the woman to listen to, she walks her talk – she has walk_ed_ her walk."

As soon as Linda left, a native man, John arrived. We were talking when Isaiah, our young sundancer friend turned up. It was a complete switch from the female energy which had just been manifested. We went into the altar, Filipe, Isaiah, John and I. Filipe asked me to play the flute for John, then he and Isaiah sang, playing the drum and rattle. The energy became intensely male, in a true ceremonial sense. I felt privileged to be there. But I was acutely aware of the need for female balance, for the healing of the female aspect of John, not just the male. I did my best to keep my heart connected to the female energy.

As John returned from his journey, Filipe told him the Grandmothers had not yet come to visit him and asked me to sing a song. He and Isaiah left the room, taking the intense male energy with them. The songs that had come through before were always soft, gentle and sweet. This was what Filipe was expecting, but this time a strong song came, a powerful woman warrior song. It was a native Grandmother's song. She sang, I felt her come and hold John as an infant, holding him, soothing him with her beauty.

Once everything quieted down, leaving Filipe and myself alone, Filipe presented me with Huichol medicine woman clothes. "I have waited a long time to gift these to some-one," he said. The bright red, patterned skirt and waist-length blue top fit perfectly, but I was a little self-conscious putting them on. Filipe looked at me firmly making me stand in front of the mirror. "You stand there until you see what I see," he told me. I stood there for a long time, until I could see myself truly, not just in medicine woman clothes, but as a medicine woman. "Those who know will know," he said.

Chapter 43

THE WOMAN'S ALTAR

It was four months before Filipe returned to Prescott. I was taking a portrait painting class with my friend Susan. We started a deep conversation about how things are moving quickly, how this is a serious time; it is time for women to rise up and come into their strength. We addressed how there is no time to waste; we need to leave the bullshit of "I can't do this," "I'm not good enough," or "I don't know enough"; there is no time for this way of thinking. I left feeling strong and determined.

I arrived home to find the altar transformed. Filipe had me close my eyes and taking me by the hand, he led me to the healing center. He sat me down on one of the Huichol women's chairs, placed a Huichol medicine woman's hat on my head, finally instructing me to open my eyes. The altar was completely re-arranged. The beaded buffalo skull was there and the beaded skull of a young deer. Above the altar was the portrait of Filipe which I had painted, depicting his relationship to the deer, the medicine, the drum and the feathers. Below that was the birthing/re-birthing yarn painting which taught me so much. There were small bottles of water gathered from the sacred springs of the Huichol arranged in a semi circle around the Hicuri medicine. In front was the picture of my grandson taken soon after his birth.

Filipe told me, "This is now a woman's altar, a re-birthing altar; this is Daisy Lucas' altar. You have walked your walk; you are now the medicine woman here." He left me to become acquainted with the new altar and to begin the understandings inherent within.

I sat a while, in gratitude, knowing I was ready to step up. I prayed, "Make me a hollow reed, a vessel, letting

225

You work as *You* want. Allow this place to be a safe place for women, where they can resonate with God's feminine energy, exquisitely reflecting their fine beauty, their true nature. I pray they feel safe to be who they truly are. I pray for many, many people to come here."

The following morning, I woke early in order to do a sunrise ceremony, praying for the guidance I needed. As the sun rose I felt the warmth penetrate my being and was assured by Spirit, "It is not so intimidating - it is not you doing it!" I had to laugh being grateful for the teaching I already knew - basically that I knew nothing. A few months later, Filipe gave me my medicine woman PHD, however, he made it clear I still had much to learn.

I had not written any of this book for a while. Spirit now instructed me to write again. I had stopped at the most difficult part for me - Alex's transplant. This time while writing I felt clear; even though I expressed the horror of children dying, I felt distant from it.

Shortly after midnight, I woke up with a sense of dread, not knowing why. I prayed for Filipe, I prayed for understanding and I prayed for the Grand Will, the absolute will of Great Spirit. I felt somewhat better, enough to allow me to get more sleep but in the morning, I was still imbalanced. I proceeded with my hundred wall squats which usually harmonizes me quickly and thought I was O.K. I went to the healing center to see Filipe, he looked at me and could tell immediately I was still not balanced. He asked if I was all right, but I knew I had to handle it on my own, telling him, "No, but it is nothing I can't deal with."

I walked outside for a while, wandering my land, connecting with the earth. As I walked, things became clear. I needed to find peace, no concern with future, past or anything else. I went deeper inside and returned to the horror of the transplant. I could see I was still traumatized.

The greatest blessing is behind the deepest pain, I knew this. Clearly, I needed the blessing, but the horror was intense forbidding me insight.

I returned to the house to practice Chi-Lel, immersing myself in the form combined with the 'three centers merge' standing meditation. I visualized inner harmony, allowing light to flow into all areas of my being. I knew Alex was alive but the trauma still remained. I shifted perspective finding there was indeed something other than tragedy and pain and upon separation from the horror, the gift showed itself. The transplant produced the absolute strength for me to stand with God, no fear, no barriers. It was the strength I exuded at that time.

The next morning three women came to the altar and to my surprise Filipe had me lie in the center. Usually I *work* at the altar and it seemed I should be giving, not receiving. He explained to the women this was now a woman's altar, but I was tired. He asked the women to pray for me. I lay there, silent tears pouring. When the tears of exhaustion eased, I began to absorb the total support of these incredible, loving women; I was renewed and strengthened.

Chapter 45

INSIGHTS AND HEALING

An acquaintance of Filipe, Cindy, visited from out of state, planning to stay a couple of weeks for healing work. Filipe asked me to take care of her by myself. I was being asked to do something unfamiliar, I needed a sureness of serene presence. I connected with her at the altar and I was aware of the many tools I had been given. I presented her with my knowledge, giving permission to use what felt best.

I informed Cindy we would come to the altar each morning, praying for daily guidance. I never know why certain things are said at the altar, but I have learned what is spoken always has a reason. I shared about having a child for another couple, how God came asking me to do this. It touched her deeply, reminding her of a significant time when she hadn't acted. She had heard, but hadn't obeyed. She comprehended her disconnection from her inner voice. She told me about an abortion she had recently and another, years before that. She felt her choice was a reason for recent difficulties and for some of her anger.

I remembered almost a year earlier, Filipe had worked with a woman, Ann, who'd had an abortion many years previously. She was able to give "birth" to this child and to accept him, allowing his spirit to be with her. I was instrumental at that time in bringing forgiveness. When I expressed this to Filipe he corrected me and showed me - No, I was the vehicle used by Great Spirit to bring the spirit of forgiveness. I recalled how Filipe had used his feathers to help the sensation of milk letting down, so this woman could experience the sensation of breast-feeding her child, nurturing his spirit.

Filipe made it clear Cindy was my responsibility so I used my intuition asking if she wanted to give birth to her aborted fetus. This was Spirit's direction. She agreed. I played the flute and prayed. As I did so, she began to feel life in her abdomen, experiencing the birth of both children. When it became obvious they were with her, I stopped playing. She affirmed, yes, indeed she was now holding both of them. She told me one was fair, the other dark. She described one, a boy, as being "so angry."

I suggested she breast-feed them both, hold them together, letting them both know they were wanted. I used the feather as I had seen Filipe do, to allow the milk to come down, allowing her to experience nurturing her children. I told her to love them, soothe them, to comfort the little boy until all his anger vanished. She did this and then she told me they left together, happy.

Cindy left a couple of days later. Though she'd had this birth experience, I felt really sad I couldn't give her more. Filipe had me sit quietly, ground myself, going deep inside. Why did I feel so bad? As I reflected more deeply, I realized it was not about Cindy but my husband, Eric. Both Eric and Cindy were dealing with anger and childhood issues. The parallel slapped me in the face. I saw I was still guilt-ridden with Eric's pain. As I went deeper still, this realization sparked my idea of letting God down. Tears silently streamed down my cheeks. I went still deeper when Spirit asked, "Did I ever ask you to heal him?" "No!" I realized. That had come from Eric himself, from a poem he had written years earlier, but it had not come from God, it had never been what Spirit asked of me. I had not let Spirit down and I had not let Eric down, I had not failed anyone. Spirit continued, "I asked you to trust him, and this you did, and this is why you can trust me now to do this work. You learned trust."

MORE LESSONS

Nina, an elderly friend was coming for a four day healing. She had been very sick having previously battled breast cancer with the help of Filipe. As she journeyed, a vision of boils rising up from her body manifested. I swept them off towards the medicine on the altar with my fan. As they touched the medicine they dissolved, making a sizzling sound.

On the second day, Filipe and I created a bed using sleeping mats making Nina more comfortable. We covered her with the deer skins and I played the flute. I sat behind her head as I played being subtly reminded of the abortions she had mentioned some time before. Spirit was telling me these children needed acceptance. The number 8 came to me symbolizing Nina needed 8 cleansings.

As I played the drum, I felt the children being born through me. As they came, I held them, breast-fed them and nurtured them. I was in the position of babysitter being reminded how I previously breast-fed children other than my own. After being nurtured, the children left. I felt sad as they went, but Filipe told me not to feel that way. He was right; I knew they had to be released happily. Filipe directed me to sing a lullaby. As I sang, the drum resonating my voice, a beautiful song came creating an idyllic place for them. They were in a meadow with deer all around. I saw them as being happy and totally free.

When Nina finished her journey, we came out to sit with Filipe, but he soon knew we had unfinished business; it was important for me to share with Nina my view point of what had happened. I learned there had been two abortions - the eight cleansings had been to introduce each of the children to the four grandparents. Nina's gratitude was necessary to complete the healing. Being seventy,

Nina had the abortions long before, never looking back with regret. As we shared, the conversation quickly turned to her older daughter, Sandra, who experienced many difficulties in her life. Nina thought she had caused these problems, creating deep trauma within her child. She was carrying huge guilt regarding this.

On the third day of Nina's healing, my eleven month old granddaughter, Ahsanya, came with her mother, Leah. It was perfect timing, as always, simply the mathematics. Nina held my granddaughter for a long time. Filipe encouraged her to hold the baby against her shoulder, gently patting her to arouse her mothering instinct.

It was time to enter the altar; Nina lay down, Leah and Ahsanya joining us. Leah took the position of midwife; I had quietly asked her if she would do this while Nina had been holding Ahsanya. My being surrogate mother was not enough; Nina needed to give birth to these two children herself. When I told Nina this she was a little surprised and said, "Only you could have said this to me, Daisy".

I played the flute giving her time to get used to the idea. After the song, she acquiesced with the statement, "Can I give birth to them both at once?" I laughed," It will be however it will be." But I sternly added it was vital for her to *want* the children. Their birthing and nurturing must take place.

Nina began to waver; it was one thing to birth them, another to *want* them. I played the flute for her again to give her time. When the song ended, I quietly spoke to her. She told me three spirits occupied her womb, filling her with great joy. She saw the two aborted souls as transparent beings. I sat behind her, reassuring her, "you are not alone this time Nina, we are here with you." I played the drum while Leah massaged her feet. The drumming intensified as the beat changed to almost a

232

heartbeat. Nina was birthing the children. Leah picked up two eagle claws giving them to Nina to hold. The drumming ended, the children birthed.

Afterwards, Nina retold her experience; when handed the eagle claws, she felt herself become an eagle, the two fetus' becoming baby eagles, flying and soaring together. Shortly thereafter the young flew on. Now it was time for her daughter, Sandra. Sandra remained in the nest. Nina had flown to hunt food for her. She remembered her daughter being young, knowing herself a good provider, a caring mother.

I was *completely* exhausted after this experience. I told Nina I needed sleep. Filipe, had gone for a drive during the healing process; as the feminine energy manifested during this work, he left. Calling on his cell phone, he instructed me to lie down on his bed for a while. I rested, praying for *all* the fetus' who had been aborted. Hundreds, maybe thousands came to me. Soon they left, happily waving goodbye. The little spirits who came to me were freed, all except for one, a little girl. I got up, and Filipe, who had since returned, had me write a letter to Nina which he dictated.

"My dear friend, dear sister, dear Mom, dear Grandmother; for you fill all those empty places in my heart." I wrote, "Today you are also my spiritual birth Mother as today in your rebirth, you birthed me as a medicine woman. Today, I understand what it is to be a medicine woman thanks to your healing. I write this letter because it would be hard to verbalize, so I let my heart speak through my pen. Today, all the pain I experienced, in all aspects of my life, was well worth the compensation of this morning's blessing.

Thanks to you, I now know my true destiny, my true purpose. Had I known the rewards, I would have gladly paid twice the price and yet I know this is simply the beginning of my birth. I, like those two little eagles, am flying free today, thanks to your courage, your willingness to go to the depths illuminating the 'blessing behind the wound' ......"

ONLY THE BEGINNING FOLKS,
ONLY THE .....

As I finished writing, a dear friend, Sheri, drove up the driveway. Her destination elsewhere, but she knew she *had* to come to the healing center. She needed to come right then. Again the mathematics. Filipe asked me to share the morning experiences with Nina and to read her the letter I had written. I ended by telling her about my prayer in the bedroom and about the child whose presence was still with me. I was trying to intellectually understand why this one didn't leave (perhaps I had miscarried a child without knowing it?), when she told us that she, too, previously had an abortion. Filipe indicated that we could take care of that now, and as Sheri and I entered the healing center, he mentioned perhaps this one was hers. Sheri lay down on the newly created birthing bed; Filipe poked his head through the door grinning as he said, "We need stirrups on this bed!" And then he left.

I talked to Sheri for a while, explaining the process I had seen others go through. I talked about how to nurture the child, how to forgive it for coming at an inconvenient time. Then I gave her time to be comfortable with what was being asked. When I stopped playing, she told me she already felt life in her womb; she could feel movement. I sat behind her, playing the drum. The drum intensified, the rhythm changing. I looked at Sheri. She moved her legs into birthing position, breathing in the manner of a woman in labor. She later shared she had literally felt cramps and pushing.

Sheri sat gently cradling her child, a child she saw, but I did not. "What do I do now?" she asked. I inquired, "What does the child want?" She said, "She is very peaceful and doesn't want to go anywhere." So I asked her what *she* wanted. I said it may be about integration rather than separation; the right words manifesting. As Sheri reflected, Spirit instructed her to open her heart (yes, it was the little girl who stayed with me), the child would do the rest.

She'd had three previous visions in the Bad Lands where she was a Native woman, pregnant, being led on the back of a horse by her husband. This same vision came strongly to her now. She knew the child she carried in her vision died. I said, "Go deeper". As she did so, she saw she had been unable to save this child. I was prompted again by Spirit to say, "Go deeper". Suddenly Sheri voiced, "*He* was not able to save the child." She realized her husband had not saved their child, this being why she never trusted men and never wanted children. She saw how this event had affected her entire life.

As she opened her heart to the child, she felt healing. As they integrated, she was delighted and excited to know her child. "I can't wait to show her my porch!" she declared. She expressed she also felt out of time as we know it, she didn't know if this life was in preparation for the other or vice versa. I expressed, there was no time, it was all one.

As she left, she went to the car, returning with a check stating, "This work MUST continue".

Janet, (a Cherokee woman) arrived along with a friend. I felt like a little kid, intimidated by her, but I didn't let my lack of confidence stop me. Janet worked with Nina as I drummed. She helps people with cancer and also listens to what she is guided to do by Spirit. When she finished, Spirit directed me to give her the drum. While Janet played, I birthed Nina. The drumming ended exactly as the birthing concluded. The birth of Nina was followed by a spiritual after-birth, connecting her directly with Spirit.

Filipe had me play the flute for a long, long time. He told me to pray for Alex during my flute playing.

The evening before, Alex had been angry and it affected me. I needed a co-parent for Alex. That morning, the weight continued to crush me. I thought balance would return at the altar after my wall squats, but as I went to see Filipe it was obvious it had not. As we talked, I said I never asked for this - I never asked to be a single parent. I realized this to be the remaining part of a need for a companion. It also came clear I felt guilty I had hung on to Alex's life so desperately. Now, I was not sure I had done the right thing. Had I forgotten it had been Alex's choice to live?

I saw clearly how Spirit had created Alex's life in me, Spirit being Alex's father, not Eric. I realized Alex's father had not walked out on him; *this* Father was always there and was co-parenting with me. I finally felt a great peace, but there was no time to indulge in it. Spirit came and told me clearly, "Now that you have worked that out, you are needed - time to get over to the altar."

I played the flute for Nina and also for my son. A beautiful prayer came through the music as it spiraled deeper and deeper. I saw Alex filled with light, I saw him as he truly is. I no longer looked at him with sadness, I no longer felt sorry for him because he lost his dad. I saw him as a complete and whole being with a wonderful future, a future formed by his own choices – his own adventure. I was filled with gratitude for his life and for his presence in mine.

AT THE SAME TIME

Filipe made eagle wing fans for the altar, attaching eagle claws. I had scheduled a class for the evening of Nina's and Sheri's births, but found I was exhausted, truly grateful only Sam showed up. I began sharing the latest happenings at the healing center with her.

Sam looked at me with tears in her eyes, divulging information only one other knew. When she was eighteen years old she had been in an abusive marriage and pregnant. Her husband, who later died in prison, had punched her in the stomach killing the baby. Sam blamed herself for not having the strength to leave him, saving her baby; though she was later able to flee, saving herself.

I told her she could give birth again and she agreed but said it would be hard; she thought she would have to re-live what had happened. I told her – "NO - that is the past; this is about giving birth as you would have wanted to, finally having a beautiful experience of birth with this child." I gave suggestions to her as to how to prepare herself and we set a time for the following week.

A few days later, Margaret who pours water for the woman's sweat lodge, came to the altar. The sweat lodge was mandated by Spirit. When she returned from her journey, Filipe told her more of what the altar was about, how he felt the problems of women came from the imbalance in men and their misuse of women. Margaret was grateful he expressed this, she mentioned her anger focused on men carelessly wasting their seed. It was women who paid the consequences on so many levels. This conversation impacted me deeply.

During my wall squats I felt myself step out of any pain caused by men; caused by Eric; my brother, my Dad.

I stepped away from feeling I was never good enough. Then it went all the way back, through my DNA to the beginning, to God; I was a whole woman.

Later I was at the altar playing the flute for Arlene. During the song, I knew stepping out of my pain was not enough, forgiveness would bring me home. I forgave Eric, my brother and my Dad. The song connected me to Mother Earth and to her healing and I understood how the healing of women is vital to the healing of Mother Earth; that it is the feminine that is becoming whole and healed.

When Sam came back the next week, she was ready and excited, lying down on the birthing bed with no hesitation. I talked to her about wanting the child and also about forgiving the child if there was anything to forgive. I played the flute for the child to come. Sam was ready, there was no need to talk, she felt her abdomen grow and her hands rest comfortably on her large belly. After the birth, she shared how she felt the presence of her ex-husband with her; she invited him to share in the birth of their child. She realized this experience was also about his healing; in fact it was mostly for him. I was moved by her pure heart and her ability to forgive.

I left the room and spoke to Filipe. He said she should use this connection to go through all of her relationships bringing forgiveness for everything done to her, forgiveness for everything done to others. I relayed this to Sam, instructing her to say this aloud, hearing it herself before letting the memory go.

While she was forgiving those who had hurt her, I became aware of my own need for forgiveness. Surprisingly, I found I needed to forgive God for asking me to give up the baby after accepting her as my own, after I allowed myself to love her. It's funny; I always thought it was me who needed to be forgiven for questioning God. I felt guilty for thinking He had asked too much of me. But in fact it was me who needed to forgive Spirit in a deep and beautiful prayer carried by the drum. It took me a few more lessons until I came to understand that no forgiveness was necessary. Spirit had only asked me to do what I had wanted to do, nothing more.

Sam shared how she felt light; she hadn't realized how much she had been carrying. Her great heart of forgiveness enabled those who came in spirit also to forgive each other. It is vital we let go of old resentments, however intense they are; they affect not only us but also our children and all of those around us. Sam taught me about the human capacity for forgiveness, if she was able to forgive what happened to her, anything can be forgiven. Sam knew her child was fine, a boy.

As we stayed together for a while, Sam expressed how she had so far to go in her journey, how I was so much further ahead. I told her this was absolutely false and I took her over to the painting I had been working on showing the three stages of woman. The child, the young woman and the grandmother depicted by the pure spirit of the Huichol. I told her it will be called, 'At the Same Time'. The words spoken told how there is no time, we are that person who is absolutely complete and whole, wise and beautiful, shining with the light of Spirit - NOW!

I said, you can plod through, or you can take a quantum leap, knowing wholeness is now and you can step into it instantaneously. "The truth is," I said, "you are everything you want to be right now, that is *all* you truly are."

She later shared one simple sentence with me. "I used to pray to feel joy - now I can."

Chapter 49

FORGIVENESS

Filipe spoke more about the need for forgiveness. This became an important part of the work happening at the healing center. Every name is written down and then the paper burned. While the list burns, one lets go of all transgressions, knowing it is done and is not to be revisited. He indicated (subtly) perhaps this was something I needed to do. For several days he was gone to the reservation and I thought it would be a good opportunity. But whenever I thought about it I talked myself out of it.

The morning after Filipe returned, I woke up knowing this was something I now needed to do without delay. I took a piece of paper, pen and lighter and walked out to my prayer rock. As I followed the familiar path, tracing the animal trails, my prayer deepened, purpose coming to me more clearly. This trip was not about being forgiven, but about forgiving.

The morning sun was beating down, the land parched in this high desert. My rock and the surrounding land welcomed me. What I needed to forgive came clear. The list was not long, the pattern obvious. These were all people who enabled me to feel less than I am, less good, less intelligent, less worthy etc. Near the end of the list the name Luke Chan came, I didn't know what I had to forgive him for - in my conscious mind, he had done nothing that needed forgiveness; but the name came in clearly, so I wrote it down with a prayer of forgiveness for whatever it was. I also forgave Filipe.

Lastly, I found I needed to forgive myself, simply for being human. How liberating! Whenever a thought or emotion came in that was not clear and aligned with Spirit, I didn't allow it to stay with me.

CHOOSE WISELY

S ome things you have to do alone and I found myself walking, with great determination, out to the sacred Huichol altar, ten thousand feet above sea level in the heart of Mexico. I was completely by myself, the trail opening before me, leading me on. It was Monday, after Easter; all the tourists had left the little town, their religious rites having reached a conclusion. It was quiet, no-one else around.

Icy moisture blew out of the clouds, chilling my body, but not my soul. Clouds kissed the earth with their gentle white touch, blanketing my view, but the path continued to open and I kept walking. My prayer needed to be taken to the sacred altar in the mountains; my flute music, my heart, the work already done at the altar in Prescott, all needed to be offered. I wanted clarity and I needed to connect directly, removing anything that was out of balance.

The medicine man had indeed passed from my life. I had learned the lessons I needed from him with new experiences opening up. Everything had to be aligned correctly. My trip to Mexico had been directed and orchestrated by Spirit, I was merely doing what my heart told me was necessary.

I continued, without slowing down, for well over two hours. At last, there were obvious signs of the altar ahead. Climbing the precipitous path around the side of the mountain, the powerful wind matched my own determined will. It was as if we climbed together. The wind no longer tried to deter me, but pushed me forwards, beckoning me, driving me safely ever upwards until the altar opened in front of me. I had arrived; completely welcomed, loved and accepted.

The fog cleared just long enough to grant me the gift of seeing the expanse of Wirikuta, far below my desolate mountain perch. I remained there - praying, offering, singing, communicating - until I was told it was time to leave. I didn't want to go but was gently told I had done what I came to do.

On the journey back, the wind whipped at my long, deep red skirt, blowing me into the spiky plants which tried to hold me; grabbing me, entangling my skirt in their spines. As I stopped to disentangle myself, I remembered the Himalayas. It was in those mountains, at this same altitude, close to Jomsom, where the wind blew with a similar intensity. I had thought "I am high enough" and had not allowed myself to step fully into the joy that was shown; somehow I thought it should belong to others yet not to me.

This time I made a different choice, I made the choice to step fully into the joy of being in the presence of Spirit. Untangling myself and once more striding down the path, I prayed for the light of my being to shine ever more brightly with each step I take. Determined that each step lead me towards greater wholeness. I choose to walk in joy and laughter knowing the gift of living on this earth.

I prayed each step and each breath be ever more sacred than the one previous; continually expanding, continually growing into the potential of everything existence can offer. I know the only limitations are self-inflicted and I no longer allow myself to become entangled in limitations and self-doubts.

Today the world began anew. We have the choice, to continue as we have been going or to wake up. Let us choose to shift, to act rather than re-act. Life can be as wonderful as we make it. Let us direct the light to illuminate our highest self. Let us choose to be actively intelligent and creatively wise, balanced emotionally, physically, mentally and spiritually.

"Where there is light in the soul,
There is beauty in the person.
Where there is beauty in the person,
There is harmony in the home.
Where there is harmony in the home,
There is honor in the nation.
Where there is honor in the nation,
There is peace in the world."

Chinese Proverb

To Contact Daisy Lucas:

Email   atthesametime@cableone.net

Website   www.atthesametime.net

LaVergne, TN USA
11 November 2010
204543LV00001B/31/P